THE SON OF PORTHOS
THE MUSKETEER

Borgo Press Translations by FRANK J. MORLOCK

Plays by ALEXANDRE DUMAS

Anthony
The Count of Monte Cristo, Part One
The Count of Monte Cristo, Part Two
The Count of Monte Cristo, Part Three
The Count of Monte Cristo, Part Four
The Last of the Three Musketeers; or, The Prisoner of the Bastille (#3)
The Three Musketeers—Twenty Years Later (#2)
Napoléon Bonaparte
Richard Darlington
The San Felice
The Three Musketeers (#1)
Urbain Grandier and the Devils of Loudon
The Whites and the Blues

Related Dramas:

The Son of Porthos the Musketeer, by Émile Blavet (#4)

THE SON OF PORTHOS THE MUSKETEER

A PLAY IN FIVE ACTS

ÉMILE BLAVET

Adapted from the Novel by Paul Mahalin

Translated by Frank J. Morlock

THE BORGO PRESS
MMXI

THE SON OF PORTHOS THE MUSKETEER

Copyright © 2004, 2011 by Frank J. Morlock

FIRST EDITION

Published by Wildside Press LLC

www.wildsidebooks.com

DEDICATION

For Conrad Cady,

*Who has encouraged and supported my work on **Dumas** for over a decade.*

CONTENTS

CAST OF CHARACTERS	9
ACT I, Scene I	11
ACT I, Scene II	36
ACT II, Scene III	65
ACT II, Scene IV	87
ACT II, Scene V	96
ACT III, Scene VI	116
ACT III, Scene VII	136
ACT IV, Scene VIII	154
ACT IV, Scene IX	173
ACT IV, Scene X	184
ACT IV, Scene XI	187
ACT IV, Scene XII	190
ACT V, Scene XIII	193
ACT V, Scene XIV	200
To Provincial Directors	213
ABOUT THE AUTHOR	214

CAST OF CHARACTERS

Joel
Aramis
Petit Renaud
King Louis XIV
Asdrubal
Bonlarron
Bistoquet
Marshal de Créqui
Pierre Lesage
Brégy
Bazin
D'Esperon (doubles First German officer)
De Champvallier (doubles Second German officer)
De Gevry (doubles An Officer)
General Schutz (could be doubled)
Boislaurier
Louvois (doubles Simon Prieur)
De Maupertius
Torgol
Chassevent (doubles First Drinker)
Vide-Gousset
Guilledon (doubles Second Valet)
Maître Lebiniou (doubles Third Valet)
Conductor of the Coach
First Chevau-Leger
Second Chevau-Leger

The Jailor
Simon Prieur (doubles Louvois)
Yves Guerin & The Major (same actor)
An Officer (doubles DeGevry)
First German Officer (doubles D'Esperon)
Second German Officer (doubles Champvallier)
A Doctor & Third Valet (same actor) (doubles Maître Lebenion)
First Drinker, Second Valet (doubles Chassevent)
Françoise D'Aubigné, widow Scarron
Aurora de la Tremblaye
Madame de Montespan
Marie Therese
Paquette
Cateau
First Gossip & First Page (same actress)
Second Gossip & Second Page (same actress)
Third Gossip

A Tailor, A Hairdresser, A Valet de Chambre, Musketeers, Bodyguards, Chevau Legers—Bombardiers, Soldiers of different corps, German Soldiers, drums, trumpets, fifes—pages, Lords, Great Ladies, men and women of the People.

Addition roles that can be doubled—General Schutz, Pierre Lesage, and Créqui—but because these parts are very important, it is essential that the actor not be recognized.

ACT I

SCENE 1

The action takes place in 1678.

The Inn of the Golden Heron in Saint Germain.

The room of the Inn—huge chimney in the back at the left. Tables. Stools.

Bonlarron, near the chimney, is overseeing the roasting of a mutton leg. Paquette is setting a table. The drinkers are seated in the back.

FIRST GROUP OF DRINKERS
Hey, Innkeeper, a jug of wine!

BONLARRON
(without budging)
See about it, Paquette.

SECOND GROUP
Innkeeper! Here—a tankard of cider!

BONLARRON
You serve, Bistoquet!

THE TWO GROUPS
Waiter! Waitress! Something to drink!

(Bistoquet runs in, bringing the jug and tankard demanded.)

BISTOQUET
Here! Here!
(stops near Paquette)
Oh! Paquette!

PAQUETTE
What?

BISTOQUET
At least tell me I am not indifferent to you.

PAQUETTE
Mr. Bistoquet, I don't know if you are indifferent to me, but when you are there, I feel nothing and when you are not there.

BISTOQUET
When I'm not there?

PAQUETTE
It's absolutely the same thing.

BISTOQUET
But I idolize you, Paquette. It's for me to approach, you who come every Sunday to help your Master Bonaventure Bonlarron, at the inn of the Golden Heron that I wear this white apron and put on this kitchen hat, insignias of my servitude! For I wasn't born a servant. I am a lyric poet. I am. And I earn my living honorably by making slogans for confectioneries and manufacturers of doggerel. And did I make slogans—here's mine—this one—Paquette—I cannot live if you're not about. My soul follows yours—step by step.

FIRST GROUP
Waiter.

BISTOQUET
Do you hear those drunks? They're calling me. You think that I am going there? Ah—don't you believe it! My heart is hotter than their throats are dry—and it will be time to moisten their throats after I've cooled my heart—by placing at your feet the love of a man, and the 300 pounds of income that I have inherited from my uncle, Eustache LePointer, who was, while living spoken of by the Prince.

PAQUETTE
Three hundred pounds will suit one nicely—but as to the rest, I need to consider—to consider a long while. Because you see, I can only love a man capable of protecting my innocence. Then, I know—my innocence—it really needs to be protected.

SECOND GROUP
Waitress!

PAQUETTE
And then I'm from a military family. My late mother was a vivandière, my father was sergeant in a battalion of the regiment of La Ferté—600 of the most handsome soldiers in France, which is why, I only want for my husband a great guy, a down right rascal, a hell raiser, who will carry me off like a grenadier.

THE TWO GROUPS
(together, rapping)
Waitress! Waiter! Innkeeper!

BONLARRON
(getting up, furious)
Ah, indeed! Who surrounds me impatience of this caliber? If you are in such a hurry as that, go elsewhere!

FIRST DRINKER
That's what we're going to do, Master Bonaventure.

SECOND DRINKER
And you won't see the color of our money for a long time.

BONLARRON
(rudely)
Show me instead that of the seams of your stockings.
(pushing them toward the door)

BISTOQUET
(also pushing them)
Cup in hand.
Not a care in the world.
Come again
Fifty years from now.

PAQUETTE
(going to Bonlarron)
What, are you sending them away, my godfather? Why it's the death of your Inn! It's not so well frequented already.

BONLARRON
Poooh! Customers like those Bourgeois soft as sheep—not one word louder than the other. Not one little quarrel. Not the least blow exchanged!

BISTOQUET
And a return as quiet as the customers.

BONLARRON
Yes—six pounds, ten sous.

BISTOQUET
(aside)

And six farthings. I am not adding the six farthings because I have them in my pocket.

BONLARRON
When formerly handfuls of gold thrown by the noblest hands in France, rolled on these tables.

PAQUETTE
Ah! Yes—when the forest of Saint Germain whose border is nearby—was the fashionable place to settle affairs of honor.

BONLARRON
(with enthusiasm)
Duels everyday—they broke each other's skulls, split each other's breasts, they chopped each other into mince meat. Ah—that was a fine time!

PAQUETTE
How I understand! Boom, bam, thrusts.

BISTOQUET
And gashes—thanks!

BONLARRON
The survivors came to my place—to each a shank on a spit—
(with melancholy)
Everyday I put that shank on the spit—but no one comes to eat it anymore—they no longer fight, they no longer kill each other—that's no way to live!

PAQUETTE
There—now that the tables are set, I am going to return to Saint Germain.

BONLARRON
You aren't going to dine with us, little one?

PAQUETTE
Impossible, godfather! It's time for the old coach and it would be too far for my feet from here to Saint Germain—where I sell milk to the strollers every evening. The crowd is such, when the court is at the Chateau, that when they embrace me, I need time to defend myself.

BISTOQUET
When they embrace you.
(taking her by the waist)
And me, Paquette, you won't let me nab you?

PAQUETTE
(disengaging herself)
No!

BISTOQUET
Shame because—love and its deep concerns leave only lilies on your complexion.

PETIT RENAUD
(in the doorway)
Don't be disturbed. Everything fine? Thanks! Just me—good folks without bothering you.

BONLARRON
My fine gentlemen.

PAQUETTE
Heavens! He is quaint, this little redhead.

PETIT RENAUD
(with volubility)
Who am I? Hey, is all you know your parish? I am Renaud, by God's blood! Renaud of good blood, Noble of Beam. They also call me Little Renaud. The devil take me if I know why! Little?

The King of France is no greater than I, still they are sure he has famous spurs on his boots! For the moment, I am greatly in need of a good meal and a good bed. Are you able to serve me one or the other?

BONLARRON
My gentleman, I have here a room, my best which will certainly suit you.

PETIT RENAUD
Marvelous! I'll take the room.

BONLARRON
That's mine, if your Lordship deigns to content himself with an excellent leg of mutton which I was keeping for myself.

PETIT RENAUD
A leg of mutton? Better and better—I'll take the leg of mutton.

JOEL
(in the doorway)
Pardon! I really hope that you will give me a slice.

PAQUETTE
Heavens, that blonde is nice.

PETIT RENAUD
Not a bite! You are going to see the appetite of my country.

JOEL
I affirm to you that the appetite of mine will not give way in any respect to yours.

PETIT RENAUD
Bragging! The devil if I leave anything but the bone of this leg of mutton.

BONLARRON
Ah! Allow me.

JOEL
Stay out of this, Mr. Innkeeper, I am taking it upon myself to make this gentleman listen to reason.

PETIT RENAUD
You?

JOEL
Me!

PAQUETTE
This is heating up. And I must leave.
(to Bonlarron)
Come on, goodbye, my cousin—
(curtsies to the two young men)
Gentlemen.
(looking at them alternatives)
This is amusing! When I look at one, I prefer the other.

(She leaves.)

PETIT RENAUD
Ah, indeed! Now what is it you want from me, friend?

JOEL
I wish, sir, if you'll permit it, to remind you of a proverb.

PETIT RENAUD
And what does this maxim say?

JOEL
That no one has the right to luxuries when others lack necessities.

PETIT RENAUD
What do you mean by that?

JOEL
Which means I would not be annoyed to honor the cuisine of our host in your company.

PETIT RENAUD
(to himself)
It seems a good devil to me—but no, I would have the air of being frightened.
(aloud)
I am grieved, but I've got the leg of mutton and I am keeping it.

BONLARRON
At last, a quarrel.

JOEL
(calmly)
Sir, you are not polite! But my gullet is too dry to show myself susceptible.

PETIT RENAUD
Not polite! God's belly! Do you, by chance, pretend to give me a lesson in politeness?

JOEL
After supper, as many lessons as you like, but mercy, let's eat first!

BONLARRON
Bistoquet, go find the object of the litigation.
(aside)
Perhaps they will massacre each other to eat it.

PETIT RENAUD
Know that I have beaten with long stick and pierced with thrusts big jolly fellows who were able to tuck me in their pockets.

BONLARRON
(rubbing his hands)
This is working—

JOEL
(impatiently)
Hey, it's not a question of your stature or of mine. It's a question of our teeth, that the two of us have of equal length.

BISTOQUET
(bringing the mutton on a skewer)
Boss, I cannot pull the skewer out.

JOEL
(pointing to the leg of lamb that Bistoquet has just placed on the table)
All the same, I do not think that you have the pretention of consuming by yourself a work of this importance.

PETIT RENAUD
And why shouldn't I consume it, if you please?

JOEL
Hell! Because there's a law which forbids it—

PETIT RENAUD
And what law is that?

JOEL
The law of capacity which says that the container must be larger than the thing contained.

PETIT RENAUD
Sir, you are insulting me once more! Yes, I am small; I ought to know it—I don't like someone trumpeting it in my ear.

(He draws his sword.)

BONLARRON
(aside)
It's working! It's working!

PETIT RENAUD
Praise God! You are going to pay me for these insults.
(he slams his sword on the table and the sword breaks)

JOEL
(laughing)
Pay? That's quickly agreed.

PETIT RENAUD
(furious)
Pay, yes, and with usurious interest.

BONLARRON
(going to take a rapier, hanging above the chimney to Petit Renaud)
My gentleman, allow me to present you Aménaïde.

PETIT RENAUD and JOEL
Aménaïde?

BONLARRON
My rapier as former sergeant in the Regiment of La Ferté.

PETIT RENAUD
I'll take Aménaïde.

BISTOQUET
But, boss, there are edicts against the duel!

BONLARRON
Certainly, there are edicts. We've lawyers got edicts. If there weren't any how would one be able to brave them?

PETIT RENAUD
Come on! En garde!

BISTOQUET
Ah! I cannot watch this!
(he leaves)

JOEL
By Jove! This will do for me!
(he takes the spit which he uses to ward off the blows of his adversary)

PETIT RENAUD
(in a paroxysms of rage)
Ah! The insolent intends to roast me!

JOEL
My word, no! I intend only to prevent you from nipping me.

(They duel.)

PETIT RENAUD
Praise God! I believe you are sparing me. We must finish this.

JOEL
That's it, let's be done with it! I ask nothing better. First of all, my stomach is famished.
(he knocks the sword from Little Renaud's hand and puts his

food on it)

PETIT RENAUD
Disarmed! Why kill me then! Kill me!

JOEL
Hey! If I were to kill you could we dine together?
(he picks up the sword and gives it to Petit Renaud)
For I hope you won't refuse me the honor of sharing with you the leg of lamb that you so long disputed with me?
(to Bonlarron)
Two place settings! Three place settings! As many as needed! I invite this gentleman—I invite the whole world.

PETIT RENAUD
(with emotion)
Sir, I was wrong. Will you pardon me and become my friend?

JOEL
Willingly. Put it there.
(he shakes Petit Renaud's hand)

PETIT RENAUD
Yei!

JOEL
Oh! Pardon!

PETIT RENAUD
Why you've got a fist strong enough to kill a cow.

JOEL
It's a family trait! Come on! To table! We will get better acquainted clinking glasses.

BONLARRON
Ah, indeed! In what mouse hole is that wretched Bistoquet crept?

BISTOQUET
(emerging from the cellar with a basket of bottles)
Here I am, boss, here I am! I'm bringing fresh wine.
To ease your pain.
Let's swim in wine.

BONLARRON
Place it there, flower of poltroonance, and go over there to take your pasture under the mouth of the chimney.
(taking back his rapier)
In company with Aménaïde.

BISTOQUET
(pointing to the two remaining bottles in the basket)
One for me and one for Aménaïde.

(They sit at the table, Bonlarron in the middle, Joel to the left, Petit Renaud to the right. They begin to eat. Bonlarron pours the drinks.)

PETIT RENAUD
To your health, my new friend.

JOEL
(raising his glass)
To yours,—Mr.—?

PETIT RENAUD
Petit Renaud d'Elicigaray, former naval officer in the LaRochelle Intendency. Ordered to Paris by Mr. de Colbert, who has deigned to inform me that he will receive me immediately on my arrival.
BONLARRON

You are going to see the minister—that's wonderful.

PETIT RENAUD
Wonderful, a minister? Not as much as all that. Mr. Colbert especially. Not withstanding not if that bogey man face—because, the Intendant, on his last trip to Paris, had explained my invention to him. "Here," he wrote, "is a nice kid with more wit in himself alone than 400 men who are no dummies." Textual, my friends! And he added, "Send me this Mr. Petit Renaud right away."

JOEL
(as he eats)
So you've invented something?

PETIT RENAUD
Not powder, no—but a means of using it. I've invented bombs and mortars, old chap.

JOEL
Bombs?

BONLARRON
Mortars?

PETIT RENAUD
The bomb is an enormous hollow bullet, filled with powder. By means of a wick, with a fuse which I adopted this projectile explodes, breaking up when it reaches its target and shatters into pieces whatever encounters its splinters.

JOEL
My compliments!

BONLARRON
Now there's an invention that will make a stir in the world.

PETIT RENAUD
No bad uproar indeed. And you, is it indiscreet to ask you what brings you to Paris?

JOEL
I've come to seek a name, a father!

BONLARRON
A name?

PETIT RENAUD
A father?

JOEL
I'm a Breton—my clothes indicate that to you. Breton from Belle Isle-en-mer.—It's there I grew up in the free and healthy air of the beaches, raised by a good old priest who tried to teach me Latin—and which he did not succeed in doing—and by an old soldier who taught me how to manage a sword.

PETIT RENAUD
And a spit! In which you are past master. God's belly, I know something about it.

JOEL
My mother, a rich farmer from the parish of Locmaria, held me in adoration. We were happy. One day I spy at the door of a cabaret a bad chap who was bullying a beggar. I used my strength to separate them, and the wretches fled, hurling in my face the word. Bastard!

PETIT RENAUD
Bastard!

JOEL
Yes, bastard! Like a maniac, I ran to my mother. Here's what

she told me. At the time Fouquet fortified Belle Isle against the forces of the King, he sent among us a lord from his entourage, a chevalier of great height and proud bearing, whose flair and golden braid caught the eye of all the women.

One evening some drunken soldiers were barring the path of a young girl who screamed for help; this Chevalier ran up and with the back of his hand, swept away the insulters. Then he took the one that he had just protected to her home. They loved each other all spring. After that, the Chevalier left for war and no news was had of him again! Still, my mother never doubted him—for she had proof of his loyalty. Poor mother! I fell to my knees before her, and we mingled our tears and our kisses!

PETIT RENAUD
Forgive me, comrade, for having awakened these memories!
(silence)

BONLARRON
(going quietly to the chimney under whose mantle Bistoquet is dozing—in a low voice)
Bistoquet!

BISTOQUET
(waking with a start)
Boss?

BONLARRON
It's night now—light the lamp.

(Bistoquet obeys.)

JOEL
What more can I tell you? When she died, my mother made me promise to dedicate all the strength, energy, and patience that I possess to find the man she had loved more than anything,

more than honor, so, I put all my clothes in a bundle, I saddled Coquette, and here I am looking for traces of my father. Oh! Not to claim my place in the Sun near him—but to ask him if he's still living—a bit of his tenderness and to bring him forgiveness from the dead.

PETIT RENAUD
But the name of this gentleman?

JOEL
My mother only knew his war name, Porthos!

PETIT RENAUD
Porthos?

JOEL
And those of three of his companions in arms to which he had sworn an attachment at all trials: Athos, Aramis and D'Artagnan!

PETIT RENAUD
Doubtless names of intrigue. So many enigmas to unravel. Ah! Your task will be so rough.

BONLARRON
Excuse me, gentlemen. Excuse me! I know the name of at least one of those three.

JOEL
Is it possible?

BONLARRON
Mr. D'Artagnan, damn it!

PETIT RENAUD and JOEL
Mr. D'Artagnan.

BONLARRON
The Captain of the Musketeers. The gentleman who used to frequent my inn, talked enough about his prowess. A hero of the finest sort, who kept his head under the great Richelieu and played under the heel of that intriguer of a Mazarin.

JOEL
And what's become of this Mr. D'Artagnan?

BONLARRON
(scratching his ear)
Ah! Now there! Since those days, perhaps he's defunct, although folks of that metal must have as many lives as a cat.

PETIT RENAUD
Hey! By God's belly! There are still musketeers and it would be devilish if they don't remember their old captain.

JOEL
You are right. But where to find Musketeers?

BONLARRON
The Musketeers are part of the King's household. They are with the King at Saint Germain.

JOEL
(with resolve)
Tomorrow I will go to Saint Germain.

(The clock is heard ringing.)

PETIT RENAUD
The two of us will go together.

BISTOQUET
(with joy)

The Angelus, boss!

BONLARRON
That's good! Light the candles—
(to Joel)
It's the hour that honest man go to sleep and your rooms are prepared.

JOEL
Then let's do—like honest men.

PETIT RENAUD
Good night, Innkeeper.

BONLARRON
Oh! I am with you. I hastened to nap, for I must rise before dawn for the arrival of the coach from Nantes. Let's go, Bistoquet, put up the bars!

BISTOQUET
Yes, boss.

BONLARRON
Allow me to light you.

PETIT RENAUD
That's it, light, Bonlarron, light the future captain of bombardiers of France.
(they al leave by the left except Bistoquet)

BISTOQUET
(sings)
The only true happiness is in a dream. I am going to sleep to find it.
(scratching noise at the window)
Clients at this house? Ah, why, no.

(they rap)
You can rap, I am not opening. For all that, the roads are well enough traveled tonight, thank you very much. They can attack you in the midst of the village just as well in the midst of the forest, and cold—brrr!
Who is it can come at such an hour? It can only be thieves!

VOICE OF BAZIN
Hola! Someone! Open up!

VOICE OF ARAMIS
Open up, or we'll break down the door!

BISTOQUET
Well! I told you so! Hush! Mouth shut! Perhaps they'll go away!
(going to the door through which Bonlarron exited, in a low voice)
Boss! Help! Robbers!
Boss!

(Bonlarron appears.)

BISTOQUET
There! There they are! They are breaking down the door.

BONLARRON
(going to the door)
Who goes there?

ARAMIS
Two travelers who are getting impatient!

BONLARRON
(to Bistoquet)
Imbecile!
(he opens)

(Enter Bazin and Aramis.)

BONLARRON
(pointing to Bistoquet who hides)
Please excuse this, poltroon! Heavens, where is he? In short, my gentlemen, at night my waiter is afraid of robbers and didn't dare open to you. That's why you had to wait.

BAZIN
That's all right. Give as your best room for milord.

BONLARRON
Each of my rooms is my best room; everything depends on the price.

ARAMIS
Eh, well, wise guy—the most expensive.

BONLARRON
The most expensive! Now Milord is talking. The most expensive and the best is mine, but I don't give that to everybody.

BAZIN
Insolent!

ARAMIS
(tossing a purse to Bonlarron)
That suffices. I'll take it. Go prepare it, and find a second next to mine for my companion.

BONLARRON
I'm running, Lordship—go ahead of me, Bistoquet.

BISTOQUET
Here I am, boss.
(aside, looking at Aramis)

He's got a proud bearing for all that.
(he leaves)

BONLARRON
(advancing a bottle and pouring)
If your lordship, while waiting—

ARAMIS
(impatiently)
I don't need anything—just my chamber right away.

BONLARRON
In a minute, Lordship.
(he leaves)

ARAMIS
(raising his voice)
Mr. Bazin.

BAZIN
Your Grace does me the honor—?

ARAMIS
You are forgetting, Mr. Bazin, that soon it will be 20 years that I've ceased to be priest of Vannes and that I've ceased to belong to the church militant, having renounced occupying myself with the salvation of others to endeavor to complete my own.

BAZIN
Then in that case it was to complete it most quickly that we left Madrid, where our life was gliding away so pleasantly, to run over hill and dale rather than indulging ourselves peacefully in prayer and repose for the few days remaining to us to spend on this earth.

ARAMIS
Few remaining days—! Speak for yourself, Mr. Bazin!

BAZIN
Still, Monsieur le Duke—

ARAMIS
Ah! Spare me titles which can attract the attention of the curious to me, and remember, that until Paris, I intend to keep the most strict incognito.

BAZIN
Then what shall I call the ambassador?

ARAMIS
Call me the Chevalier d'Herbalay, as before.

BAZIN
(joining his hands)
The Chevalier d'Herbalay! Good God! Truly, why doesn't Milord resume his habits, his cassock and his title of musketeer at once?

ARAMIS
(with melancholy)
No! Aramis is dead! Dead with his three companions, his true friends, his three brothers! Dead with Athos, with Porthos, with D'Artagnan!
(dully)
I repeat to you, that for the moment, I only wish to be the Chevalier d'Herbalay.

BAZIN
(with emotion)
May the will of the Chevalier be accomplished.

BONLARRON
(entering with Bistoquet)
If Milord will give himself the trouble—

ARAMIS
Let's go.

(Bonlarron lights them out.)

BISTOQUET
As for me, I'm putting up the bars! I'll hardly be able to get two hours sleep before the arrival of the coach from Nantes, and I intend to profit by it! All we need is for other robbers to come—no, other travelers! Ah, no, indeed!

BLACKOUT/CURTAIN

ACT I
SCENE 2

The coach from Nantes.

The exterior of the preceding scene. A square to the left, the Inn of the Golden Heron. To the right, the forest—night.

Asdrubal and his companions enter furtively from the right rear. The Captain and Torgol come forward. The other three groups at the back and hand shading over their eyes look off to the left.

ASDRUBAL
Hola. House.

(Mute play. Bistoquet opens the door, lets out a scream and shuts the door.)

BISTOQUET
(opening the door again, cautiously)
Huh? Who goes there?
(aside)
Wow! Villainous faces!
(he makes a movement to renter)

ASDRUBAL
(grabbing him and preventing him from reopening the door)

We have to chat.

BISTOQUET
The two of us?

ASDRUBAL
(presenting the barrel of his pistol)
All Three!

TORGOL
(on the other side, with a musket)
All four!

BISTOQUET
Yoi!

ASDRUBAL
You as the master of the hostel?

BISTOQUET
Waiter only, sir, simple waiter.

ASDRUBAL
(pointing to the house)
How many people do we have in there?

BISTOQUET
Well, there's me first of all.

ASDRUBAL
And then?

BISTOQUET
(with fear)
And then, the Boss.

ASDRUBAL
And then?

BISTOQUET
And then, two travelers arrived from the provinces.

ASDRUBAL
And then?

BISTOQUET
And then, an old lord and his valet even older then he.

ASDRUBAL
And then?

BISTOQUET
That's all!

ASDRUBAL
And what are these four travelers doing at the moment?

BISTOQUET
What are they doing? At four in the morning? It's my opinion they are sleeping, the boss having given his best room to each!

ASDRUBAL
Well, get this: If they wake up, you are a dead man!

BISTOQUET
Dead!

ALL
Dead!

ASDRUBAL
You understand? Yes? Then? Then hurry to go do as they are

doing—and with both your ears!

BISTOQUET
Impossible, my gentlemen! Here's the coach from Nantes! Wait, do you hear the coach bells shivering? Not as much as I am, still! It comes from that direction and the travelers are accustomed to refreshing themselves at our inn—

ASDRUBAL
Well! You will lock it!

BISTOQUET
But—lord—

ASDRUBAL
(abruptly)
Ah! No remarks.
(pointing to his pistol)
I have a comrade here who doesn't like them!

TORGOL
(same byplay with his musket)
Who doesn't like them, that's certain!

ASDRUBAL
So go back into your shell—and play dead, if you value your life.

BISTOQUET
(aside)
If I value it! Does one ask questions like that?

ASDRUBAL
Get going!

TORGOL
(pushing him)
Get going!

(Bistoquet reenters and can be heard bolting the door.)

CHASSEVENT
(n the distance)
Alert, Captain.

VIDE-GOUSSET
Here's the coach!

GUILLEDON
The travelers are getting out to climb the side on foot.

ASDRUBAL
That's fine, my braves! Let's take our combat posts.

(They go into ambush behind trees.)

MAÎTRE LEBINIOU
(mopping his face)
Oof! The climb was rough and the day will be hot.

SIMON PRIEUR
Happily, we are going to be able to refresh ourselves.

YVES GUERIN
And take refreshments at the same time.
(they head towards the inn)

ASDRUBAL
(barring their passage)
Excuse me!

MAÎTRE LEBINIOU
(recoiling)
Who's that?

SIMON PRIEUR
A bloke whose appearance is against him!

ASDRUBAL
(bowing to them)
Gentlemen, please consider me the most humble, the most obedient, the most devoted of your servants.

MAÎTRE LEBINIOU
Sir, it's we who are yours.

ASDRUBAL
(still bowing)
The Chevalier Asdrubal de Cordeboeuf, Colonel in the service of His Majesty—when I say Colonel, it's a figure of speech. Colonel or Captain, the grade doesn't matter. And my word, I would be very much prevented from being precise, seeing that my regiment, my company, if you like, is for the moment composed of only four gallant chaps that I have the honor to present to you—Torgol, my lieutenant, Chassevent, my standard bearer, Vide-Gousset, my quartermaster and Guilledon, my trumpeter!

SIMON PRIEUR
(shivering)
What names!

YVES GUERIN
And what mugs!

ASDRUBAL
My cadre will be complete when I've recruited some men, and

to recruit, I don't merely lack equipment. That's why I've solicited and obtained from the Provost, the commission to escort and protect honest folks traveling in the province.

MAÎTRE LEBINIOU
What! You are here to—

ASDRUBAL
To accompany you right up to the gates of Paris, and to defend you if need me, against all vexations, and criminal exigencies or culpable enterprises.

TRAVELERS
(with relief)
Ah! Truly.

ASDRUBAL
And that, in consideration of slight royalty whose figure is left to your good pleasure.

TRAVELERS
Oh! Oh!

ASDRUBAL
Only so as to restrain the generosity of my clients, I've had to resolve to tax them according to their appearance.

SIMON PRIEUR
(being difficult)
And if we don't chose to be escorted and protected?

YVES GUERIN
If we don't agree to purchase the honor of your company?

ASDRUBAL
In that case, I won't answer for your precious persons! There are

so many rogues in the country.

(He makes a sign. His companions prime their muskets.)

MAÎTRE LEBINIOU
(hastily)
Mr. Captain, we are ready to pay—

ASDRUBAL
About time.
(to the conductor of the coach)
You—come forward, take your scriblings and call the roll.

CONDUCTOR
(reading from the leaf)
Maître Lebiniou from Nantes, royal attorney.

ASDRUBAL
Men of the law and men of the sword are men of the King. Maître Lebiniou will therefore be happy to contribute a 100 pistoles for the equipment of my soldiers.
(placing his hat on the ground)
Here's my bureau of receipts, gentlemen, pass to the cash box! To you the honor, dear sir! Next!
(the lawyer places his offering in the hat)

CONDUCTOR
Simon Prieur, ship owner from Paiembeouf—

ASDRUBAL
One hundred pistoles as well. I won't do a notable merchant the insult of esteeming him less than the man of the law.
(the shop owner pays)
Next?

CONDUCTOR
Yves Guerin, sardine merchant at Croisie.

ASDRUBAL
Fifty pistoles—the fishing is excellent this year.
There—do we still have someone on your list?

CONDUCTOR
There are only two ladies: Miss Aurora de Tremblaye and—

(Joel and Petit Renaud appear at the Inn window.)

ASDRUBAL
Fine, some dowager, no doubt and her servant. Make these ladies get out.

AURORA
(at the coach door)
We are here!

(She opens the door, she advances towards Asdrubal. The other lady who has the appearance of a little bourgeois, but who is veiled, gets out behind her.)

AURORA
(giving a purse to Asdrubal)
Sir, here's what you are waiting for.

(As Asdrubal is about to take the purse, Joel has just appeared in the doorway of the Inn, grabs it and places himself between Asdrubal and Aurora.)

JOEL
(to Asdrubal)
Keep your paws down!

JOEL
(returning the purse to Aurora)
Ladies, you shall not pay ransom to this miscreant! I oppose it! Take back your purse, Miss.

ASDRUBAL
Help me, the rest of you, get your muskets.
(the bandits take aim at Joel)

AURORA
(terrified)
Sir! Oh, Sir, watch out!

JOEL
Leave me alone! Here's my shield.
(he seizes Asdrubal, he pushes him in front of him with the force of a blow from his fist, and uses him like shield)
And now, fire if such is your wish.

ASDRUBAL
Eh! Don't shoot, what the devil!
(the bandits raise their muskets)

JOEL
(to Asdrubal)
Keep quiet or I'll strangle you!

PETIT RENAUD
(coming down the steps from the inn; to the bandits)
And you, my lads, a deal: there's a charge, right, in each of your blunderbusses? Well, I'll buy all four of them from you.

ALL THE BANDITS
You will buy them from us?

TORGOL
How much?

PETIT RENAUD
All the gold appearing in this hat.

TORGOL
What?

PETIT RENAUD
Only discharge your muskets for me in this bird of passage that I went by, and I will abandon the cash to you.

JOEL
Otherwise, I'll wring the neck of your captain and I'll use his carcass to beat all of you.

TORGOL
Bargain concluded.
(he fires into the air, the others imitate him)

PETIT RENAUD
(pushing the hat with his foot)
To you, the hoard)

TORGOL
Meaning to me—to me alone.

VIDE-GOUSSET
Brigand.

CHASSEVENT
Villain.

GUILLEDON
Swine!

(at the uproar of the Musketeers, Aurora feels ill, Joel as he rushes to her releases Asdrubal)

ASDRUBAL
Thief!
(he rushes with his three companions in pursuit of Torgol)

AURORA
Miss.

PETIT RENAUD
(following the bandits with his eyes)
Charming! Delightful! The robber is robbed!

MAÎTRE LEBINIOU
And it's our money dancing off!

SIMON PRIEUR and YVES GUERIN
(groaning)
Our money! Our poor money!

VEILED LADY
Help, gentlemen, run to the Inn.

(Bonlarron and Bistoquet emerge from the Inn followed by Aramis and Bazin.)

BONLARRON
Finally, they've gone.

BISTOQUET
Now we are delivered!

ARAMIS
(in the doorway)
What's going on, anyway? Shots—this young girl.

JOEL
My God—wounded perhaps!

ARAMIS
Let's see about this.
(going to the young girl)
No, no, sir—don't worry; Miss has only fainted.

JOEL
Fainted!

PETIT RENAUD
No question, a syncope, caused by fright.

ARAMIS
(to Bazin)
My flash! Quickly—my travel case.

(Bazin goes in.)

SIMON PRIEUR
To make her come to, tell me about a good glass of hot wine.

YVES GUERIN
(emphasizing)
With four spices and a bit of pepper.

MAÎTRE LEBINIOU
As for me, I am for simple and economical remedies—nothing's better than a pot of fresh water across the face.

(Bazin emerges from the Inn with a flask.)

PETIT RENAUD
(making Aurora breathe it)
She, she's opening her eyes.

JOEL
(aside)
How pretty she is!

PETIT RENAUD
(to Joel)
Hey, comrade, watch out for the lightening bolt

AURORA
(weekly)
The uproar of this explosion, a bullet that I heard whistle past my ears!

ARAMIS
(to Joel)
A nervous crises—all she needs is calm.
(to the veiled lady)
I confide Miss, to your care. Lead her into a room where she can take some rest.

VEILED LADY
If you permit, Miss—

BISTOQUET
I am going to lead you—

AURORA
(rising to Aramis)
Truly, sir, how can I thank you?

ARAMIS
Go, my dear child, and finish pulling yourself together. You'll be advised of the coach's departure—only then will I permit you to thank me for a service that any gallant man would have rendered you in my place.

(Aurora, leaning on the veiled lady and heading toward the inn, Joel accompanies her up to the door. Before entering, she turns toward him, extending her hand.)

AURORA
Thanks, sir!

JOEL
(confused, kissing Aurora's hand)

Oh, Miss!

AURORA
(without withdrawing her hand)
Would you tell me your name?

JOEL
(moved)
Joel!

AURORA
(looking at him for a moment, then withdrawing her hand)
Thanks, Mr. Joel, thanks—!

(She goes into the Inn. Joel follows her with his eyes)

PETIT RENAUD
(to Joel)
All my congratulations!

JOEL
(dragging Petit Renaud away)
Come, Petit Renaud, come, my friend! Let's distance ourselves, were it only for a moment. I am happy, and I want to be able to say so! I want to be able to shout it! Come!

(They leave.)

ARAMIS
(who has followed them with his eyes)
Some Breton younger brother who's coming to seek his fortune in Paris.

BAZIN
(who's been chatting with the travelers)
So you've been stopped by a troupe of highway men?

MAÎTRE LEBINIOU
Stopped, attacked, despoiled!

BAZIN
And you didn't defend yourselves?

MAÎTRE LEBINIOU
Ah! Sir, it's not our job to be brave.

BONLARRON
(on the steps)
The collation awaits the travelers.
(all enter, Aramis remains)

YVES GUERIN
(heading towards the Inn)
We are honest merchants who avoid brawls and scuffles.

SIMON PRIEUR
You may be sure that if I'd had at hand a workman from my building or an employee from my office, I wouldn't have hesitated to get him killed!

(Boislaurier arrives on horseback and tosses his reins to a stableboy.)

ARAMIS
Boislurier, at last!

BOISLAURIER
Duke—

ARAMIS
(to Bazin)
Watch so that no one comes to disturb us.
(to Boislaurier)
If you please, we shall remain here.
(pointing to the inn)
There's too big a crowd in there!

BOISLAURIER
I am at Your Excellency's orders. The King's confessor had informed me that before entering Paris Your Excellency would stop at the last relay to wait for news.

ARAMIS
Are you bringing me any?

BOISLAURIER
Some very grave! Miss Fontange is dead!

ARAMIS
Dead!

BOISLAURIER
Alas.

ARAMIS
At 22! That's frightful! That's impossible!

BOISLAURIER
The poor woman succumbed to the consequences of three

equally fatal imprudences. The first was, knowing Mme de Montespan, to insult the Marquise's pride with all the dazzle of her triumphs. The second, having braved her thus, was to take into her service a certain Pierre Lesage, who came from the house of her vindictive rival—

ARAMIS
(aside)
Pierre Lesage—

BOISLAURIER
The third, accepting a glass of milk from the hands of this man.

ARAMIS
Pierre Lesage, before having been in the home of LaMontespan, was in the home of LaVoisin! Oh! Oh! Do you know what a terrible accusation you are formulating there, Boislaurier?

BOISLAURIER
I'm not the one formulating it, Duke—it's public opinion. It's the inquest which is proceeding under Mr. LaReynie, president of the Chambre Ardente—the consequences of this inquest have been such that the king must have resigned himself to break off—

ARAMIS
What do you mean?

BOISLAURIER
Pierre Lesage is in the Bastille, and Mme Montespan must no longer be at Saint Germain.

ARAMIS
Eh! What! The favorite—

BOISLAURIER
Has received an order to leave the court.

ARAMIS
Transitory exile!
(shrugging his shoulders)
She'll be back, by Jove! This crime of which they accuse her, she will scream very loudly that jealousy made her commit it. Men gladly forgive sins which they are the cause of—and before a woman, Louis, who takes himself for a God, is more a man than other men. If we are not careful, Boislaurier, within a month, he will have forgiven everything and you will see the proud Athénaïs more powerful than ever!

BOISLAURIER
So powerful indeed that the United Provinces and the Empire thought they must treat her with ambassadors.

ARAMIS
What are you saying?

BOISLAURIER
I am saying that Orange and the Court of Vienna have conferred with La Montespan, and whispered preliminaries to peace.

ARAMIS
Peace! They are going to sign a peace treaty?

BOISLAURIER
So much so that the town of Niemiegen has been designated to serve as the meeting place of the plenipotentiary.

ARAMIS
Boislaurier, what they are meditating cannot be and shall not be. France is my country, it's true, but Spain is my adopted land. It was Spain that received me when, proscribed and fugitive,

Louis XIV had placed me under the ban of the Kingdom. It's Spain that made me Duke of Alaméda, which conferred greatness on me, which confided in me the care of its interests near the office of Saint Germain. I won't suffer that my second master be humiliated! A bit for him—much for me! Besides, think that an alliance with the Calvinists of Holland, and the Lutherans of Germany would strike a terrible blow to the Company of Jesus.

BOISLAURIER
I think that you, and I, Duke, share the same apprehensions. But how to prevent it?

ARAMIS
My God! That poor Fontanges was a precious instrument in our hands. The instrument is broken another must be forged! We will be at the Marquise with her own weapons, by opposing against her, in the king's heart, a creature more enchanting than her predecessor, and no less docile to our instructions, no less devoted to our plans.

BOISLAURIER
(shaking his head)
Still, consider that all the beauties of the court have already submitted to the power of this capricious monarch.

ARAMIS
So, it will not be in the court that I will seek this enchantress.

BOISLAURIER
Where will you find her in that case?

ARAMIS
I don't know—but from the moment that I need her, I will find her.

BOISLAURIER
May God hear you!

ARAMIS
Silence! Someone is coming!

(Joel has entered form the back with Petit Renaud. The veiled lady comes down the steps from the Inn. Aramis continues to talk in whispers with Boislaurier.)

JOEL
(noticing the veiled lady)
Ah, Madame—Miss Aurora?

VEILED LADY
Ms. Aurora is in perfect health.
(low)
Get rid of your friend.

JOEL
Petit Renaud.

PETIT RENAUD
Suffice. I understand.
(goes into the Inn)

JOEL
Is Miss Aurora—?

VEILED LADY
(mimicking him)
Miss Aurora. It's not a question of Miss Aurora, but of me—

JOEL
Of you?

VEILED LADY
I'm not coming from Nantes, like Miss de la Tremblaye, but only from Rambouillet. That means I don't know this young girl.

JOEL
Still—

VEILED LADY
Yes, I profited by a mistake of those highway men that your courage put to flight, an error that, thanks to my outfit, all the world here has also shared. I consented to pass for the servant, the companion of Miss de Tremblaye, and I've already excused myself to her—I also want to excuse myself to you, so as to be able to thank my savior.

JOEL
Savior is a very big word, Madame. The old soldier, who took the place of my father always repeated this to me, "At any time when you are present and some lack respect for ladies, remember that the sword of a cavalier must emerge from its sheath all alone." And you see, I didn't even have need of my sword.

VEILED LADY
Sir, I am no less grateful to you for it, Mr. Joel, for, without you, I would have been at great risk of being recognized.

JOEL
Recognized?

VEILED LADY
And I confess to you, I was greatly in fear of it. That's why without hesitation, I accepted for a moment the role that chance gave me with Miss de Tremblaye—for I am not accustomed to travel the great highway and necessarily there was a powerful

motive.

JOEL
A love affair, I bet.
(gaily)

VEILED LADY
Bet and you will lose! No, sir—it's really much more serious. I was returning—but I must not confide my secrets to you.

JOEL
No one will keep them better than I, Madame.

VEILED LADY
I am sure of it and I am going to prove to you how great my confidence in you is. I was returning then to have my cards read by a renowned prophetess, who, expelled from Paris, has taken up refuge in Rambouillet, in that ruins of a dungeon built by Richelieu.

JOEL
A sorceress—I understand, like us.

VEILED LADY
Then you believe in the predictions of sorceresses—?

JOEL
Yes, I believe in it? I'm a Breton—and what did this fortune teller tell you?

VEILED LADY
How was it she knew the entire past of this woman who came to consult her hidden under the dress of a little bourgeoisie? How did she know that I was born in a prison, that, still a child, my parents, obliged to expatriate themselves, sent to me to the colonies where I grew up in shame and trouble? That returning to

France, destiny made me marry a sick old geezer, nailed into his armchair by paralyses? How, I say, was this woman not unaware of all the cruel trials that I forced myself to forget?

JOEL
There—she must have had all that in her cards or in your hand.

VEILED LADY
No, since she refused to examine my hand—and since she hadn't even spread her pack of Tarot when she cried out, "Your troubles are nearly over. You will emerge from obscurity under a ray fallen from the crown of France. A great monarch will love you—you will be queen—

JOEL
Queen of France?

VEILED LADY
Superstitious as I am, this prediction made me smile! But if, though impossible, it was realized, count on my protection, Mr. Joel. Meanwhile, if as small as I am, I can be useful to you—I am trying to say to you—if you are pleased to use my weak credit, don't hesitate. You will always find me ready to serve you. I dwell in the Rue Saint Antoine facing Saint Paul's church. My name is Françoise d'aubigné, widow of Scarron—governess of the royal children of France.

JOEL
(bowing)
Madame, I thank Providence for placing me in your path.

FRANÇOISE
Goodbye, Mr. Joel and believe me to be your friend.

JOEL
Ah, Madame, this friendship you are offering me with such

good grace—

FRANÇOISE
Well?

JOEL
Would you allow me to call on it immediately?

FRANÇOISE
Very willingly—what do you wish? Speak!

JOEL
For myself, nothing! Young, a good sword at my side—what do I need? Whereas she—

FRANÇOISE
She—!

JOEL
(forcefully)
The person for whom I implore your assistance, I swear to you will never know of our conversation. An hour ago, we were unknown to each other. Perhaps I will never see her again? But this meeting of a moment sufficed to decide my entire life! She has entered, the fugitive image, the sweet vision hardly seen! She will never leave it, except with my last breath.

FRANÇOISE
Why this is a passion! And for that the vision to make itself a woman and this woman were to be yours you would give—

JOEL
All that I have—no big thing—my life!

FRANÇOISE
Plague! Handsome Amadeus—it won't do to touch your idol.

JOEL
I don't know what the future has in store for us—but what I do know is that I will kill the King himself, if he wanted to do harm to Miss Aurora.

FRANÇOISE
(aside)
Now that's how I would like to be loved!

JOEL
Madame, did you see how reserved she is, almost sad? Love is a great prophet and I prophesize her poverty and misfortune. So young. Alone on the highways! What's she going to do in Paris? Seek support for her weakness, no question! She's got too much dignity, that can be read in her eyes—to ask for that support. You are offering yours to me? But I am armed against betrayals. Would you bring it to this defenseless child? Would you?

FRANÇOISE
You've got a brave heart, Mr. Joel—I promise to be the friend of the one you love, and who will one day love you—

JOEL
Ah, Madame!

FRANÇOISE
Why not? Sincere love commands love! Go on, rely on me! We still have two good hours before entering Paris—that's more than required to give you proof of my friendship.

(During this dialogue, Aramis and Boislaurier have been chatting at the back, appearing and disappearing through the trees.)

(Noise of bells, Bonlarron and the travelers emerge from the Inn.)

MAÎTRE LEBINIOU
Do you hear all this ringing? They're going to leave.

YVES GUERIN
Finally we're going to get back on our way.

(They go back.)

YVES GUERIN
(to Petit Renaud)
By Jove, my host; you have a rich food set up.

PETIT RENAUD
(compliantly)
Yes—the box is solid. And I was going to set myself to it when they made me leave the table.

BONLARRON
You were going to set to it! Well—what is it you were setting yourself to do?

PETIT RENAUD
I'd really like you to see me.

BAZIN
(low to Aramis)
Miss de la Tremblaye wishes to present her respects to the Chevalier.

AURORA
(entering behind Bazin and Aramis)
Sir, they've just informed me that we are on the verge of departure and you mustn't think, I hope, that I was going to separate from you, without thanking you, from the depths of my soul, for the care you've lavished on me.

ARAMIS
Miss, I am well paid for that care, whose merit you exaggerate—from the satisfaction I'm experiencing to see that it has been able to be of use to you—But would you, by chance be related to the Marquis de Tremblaye, who was Captain of the Guards under the late King?

AURORA
I am his great niece, sir!

ARAMIS
An excellent gentleman on my word!

CONDUCTOR
(at the rear)
Passengers, in carriage!

(Aramis escorts Aurora to the coach).

AURORA
(to Joel, who is in her path)
Mr. Joel, I am saying goodbye to you—and I wish you good luck!

JOEL
(low, bowing)
Listen carefully to your companion; she's a friend.

AURORA
(curtseying to Aramis)
Chevalier—

ARAMIS
(bowing)
Miss—

FRANÇOISE
(aside, before getting into the carriage, watching Joel follow Aurora with his eyes)
It's a shame—but I don't have the time to delay—I am going where destiny shoves me—I will keep my word to this Joel—for it's not through him that I will let myself be caught napping—!

ARAMIS
Bazin! Horses to my carriage right away!
(to Boislaurier)
We are going to start for Paris—It's important that we arrive before this young girl.

BOISLAURIER
This young girl?

ARAMIS
Bow very low to her, as will the whole Court, very soon. For this Miss de la Tremblaye, this provincial girl of whose existence Paris and Saint Germain are unaware is the woman I've chosen as the instrument of my plans—it's she who will reign over Louis the Great! It's she who will be the virtual Queen of France.

(Joel has assisted Françoise and Aurora to climb into the coach. The young girl in the coach door addresses a last greeting to Aramis. Aramis and Boislaurier bow. The carriage begins to move.)

CURTAIN

ACT II
SCENE III

The Terrace of Saint Germain.

To the right, the pavilion of Henry IV—at the back—the parapet of the terrace, with Paris in perspective. To the left, the beginning of the park.

The characters are strolling and chatting in groups at the front of the stage. Elsewhere, musketeers are on guard duty in front of the pavilion. At the back heading towards the park, passing by, alone and in groups, lords and ladies of the court.

D'ESPERON
Yes, gentlemen, I've seen with my own eyes the carriages of the Marquise taking the road to Clagny.

DE GEVRY
And this morning, with my own ears, I had His Majesty say to Père Bourdalene who greeted him when he rose. "Well, Father, are you satisfied? Mme de Montespon is leaving tomorrow for her domains."

D'ESPERON
And what did the eminent preacher reply?

DE GEVRY
That God would be even more satisfied if Clagny was sixty leagues from Saint Germain.

DE CHAMPVALLIER
While waiting, here we are rid of this marvel of marvels—marvel of arrogance.

DE GEVRY
Marvel of hissy fits.

D'ESPERON
Marvel of perfidy—

DE GEVRY
Hum! Rid of her—! Not yet! Since it is only tonight, at the Queen's gambling table, that she must officially take her leave of Their Majesties

BRÉGY
But the cause of this disgrace, tell me of it, at least, I know nothing of the intrigues of the court.

DE CHAMPVALLIER
My poor Brégy, go ask Mr. de LaReynie who's strolling over there with Mr. de Maupertius, the Captain of the Guards.

BRÉGY
LaReynie!

D'ESPERON
(emphasizing)
LaReynie, the President of the Chambre Ardente, an exceptional tribunal, instituted to investigate this Affair of the Poisons which has shocked all Paris!

BRÉGY
What! It may be true that Miss de Fontange?

DE GEVRY
Seek who profits by the crime!

DE CHAMPVALLIER
In any case—there's an open successor—

D'ESPERON
Actually, two!

BRÉGY
What succession, if you place?

D'ESPERON
Eh! That of this poor Fontange who is in the cemetery and that of this proud Athénaïs who's on the road to exile.

DE CHAMPVALLIER
The brigadier is always late!

BRÉGY
(excitedly)
And you think there can be found in the court a woman capable of causing this new chagrin to the Queen?

DE GEVRY
Oh! Oh! Oh!, no, my brave Brégy—not one, but all!

D'ESPERON
Gentlemen, here is His Majesty emerging from his apartments.
(general excitement)

(Everyone goes toward the King. Aramis in court costume, the golden fleece on his neck, enters from the left, stopping for a moment to receive the respects from ladies and cavaliers who meet him. Brégy goes toward the pavilion.)

DE CHAMPVALLIER
(to Gevry)
Tell me, Gevry, you who know everybody, who is that old Lord on whom they are lavishing all these marks of respect.

DE GEVRY
Ah! By Jove! He's wearing our cassock—have you heard tell of four musketeers, who under the late King, in the time of the youth of our old Brégy, displayed the legendary prowess of the four sons of Aymon? Well, that old geezer is the last survivor of them. Entered into orders much later, and made bishop of Vannes, he was one of the conspirators who undertook, 20 years later, to destroy Louis XIV to the benefit of his twin brother who resembled him miraculously.

DE CHAMPVALLIER
The man the iron mask—

D'ESPERON
Why wasn't he pursued by this chief?

DE GEVRY
He took refuge in Spain, where after a number of years, he became ambassador of His Majesty, Charles II.

DE CHAMPVALLIER
And Louis pardoned him?

DE GEVRY
What do you want? Reason of State? The necessity of Madrid! And then, they say, because this old musketeer is obeyed by numerous affiliates of the Company of Jesus.

D'ESPERON
In that case, let's greet him gentlemen! Greet him with a deeper bow than to Louis himself! The Sun King, indeed, reigns only in France—while the General of the Jesuits, damn it all—governs the world.

(They go to rejoin the courtiers. Those remain at the rear. Aramis, noticing Boislaurier enter heads toward him.}

ARAMIS
Well—that young girl?

BOISLAURIER
Installed in the home of the little bourgeoisie in the coach from Nantes—who is no other than the widow Scarron.

ARAMIS
Not possible!
(great commotion in the rear)
See about that, Boislaurier.

BOISLAURIER
(getting a better look)
No question it's the King who now comes this way.
(explaining)
Ah!

ARAMIS
Well?

BOISLAURIER
Here they are—the two of them!

ARAMIS
On my soul, Boislaurier, Providence is with us—for she has already done half our work.

(The whole court comes forward and arranges itself to the right and left of the King's progress. Françoise and Aurora are at the extreme right; Aramis and Boislaurier at the extreme left; Louis XIV emerges from the pavilion, followed by Maupertius. Musketeers are ranged in the back, present arms under the command of Brégy.)

THE KING
Hats, gentlemen!

(Everyone places his hat on. Louis alone remains uncovered. He bows to the ladies.)

THE KING
Ladies, I greet you.
(noticing Françoise)
Oh, it's you, Madame?
You have something to request of us?

FRANÇOISE
Sire, the most devoted of your servants wants nothing more than to present to Your Majesty the expression of boundless gratitude for the new favor which she's just received.

THE KING
Madame, I made you Marquise because I was grateful for the care with which you've surrounded my children.

FRANÇOISE
Since the King deigns to encourage me, since he allows me to importune him once again for a person worthy in all respects of his sovereign solicitude.
(Louis gestures for her to continue)
Sire, here's Miss de la Tremblaye, the daughter of your former servants, who is coming to place herself under the safeguard of your justice—

THE KING
My justice?

FRANÇOISE
Sire, Miss de la Tremblaye is an orphan and they are disputing her paternal inheritance!

THE KING
Another young girl who has come to Paris to litigate! It's a very arduous task you are undertaking, Miss!

FRANÇOISE
It has to be done, Sire!

AURORA
Oh, don't believe that it's from cupidity! My parents, that heaven has taken from me, have left me only a name without blemish. God is my witness, if I were alone, I would content myself with this inheritance. For noble girls without fortune there is always an open refuge—the convent!

THE KING
The convent. That would be a great misfortune.

AURORA
But I am the head of family, Sire. I have charge of souls. I have a young brother and a very small sister! And its' for them I am doing my best to fight.

THE KING
That's fine, Miss, that's very fine. There's the good fight! And I am announcing to you that beginning today, you have the King of France as your ally.

AURORA
Oh, Sire—how much goodness!

THE KING
Don't thank me! It's the duty of a prince to watch over his subjects.
(handsomely)
This duty is sweet to me to fulfill when it has for its object the daughter of one of my gentlemen, and one of the most accomplished persons whom it was given me to admire at my court.

(Aurora lowers her eyes.)

FRANÇOISE
All that remains is for me to obtain the King's permission to go rejoin my pupils.

THE KING
We will give you leave until tomorrow, Madame. It pleases us for you to appear at our reception this evening.

You will bring your charming protégée there. I want to direct the Queen's benevolence to her.
(raising her voice)
Gentlemen, we set you all at liberty!
(general commotion of leaving)

DE GEVRY
Did you notice what warm attention the King gave to that little girl?

D'ESPERON
Perhaps she's a rising star?

DE CHAMPVALLIER
If Brégy were there—we could tell him the succession has already taken place.
(the courtiers reach the rear and disperse bit by bit)

(At a gesture from Aramis, Boislaurier has departed by the left. Louis XIV watches Aurora who is leaving with Françoise—Aramis approaches him.)

ARAMIS
(low)
What a charming young girl—right, Sire?

THE KING
(turning)
Señor d'Alaméda!
(haughtily)
Sir, I think you are interrogating me—?

ARAMIS
(bowing)
Please God that I am not forgetting respect to such a degree. I only thought myself able to translate the thought I read on your august face. May the King pardon me if I've been wrong or if I am mistaken.
(he makes a face as if to retire)

THE KING
Stay, sir—! Just as well, I am tepidly satisfied by the attitude of your government in the conferences at Niemiegen

ARAMIS
Ah!

THE KING
Yes, Spain is making common cause with England and the Empire—

ARAMIS
Sire.

THE KING
In truth, like Charles II, your master; like the Emperor and his ministers, such great protectors of the Prince of Lorrain—do they think I am so little capable of seeing the interests of France? Nancy restored to the future brother-in-law of Leopold of Austria! That would be to open the gates of Vincennes to Croats and brutes! Let's not speak of it any further. I've taken Lorrain and I'm keeping it.

ARAMIS
Sire, there's a much more important point that His Catholic Majesty has directed me to call to the attention of Your Most Christian Majesty.

THE KING
And what's that?

ARAMIS
Is Your Majesty cognizant that the Protestants of his kingdom are leagued in intelligence with their co-religionists in Holland and the Rhineland? Does He know that, in their temples, they are preaching calls to a pretended universal peace, which is the negation of sovereign rights and national frontiers? That they are opening colleges, funding hospitals, establishing manufacturers, printing books and proclaiming in their conventicles while they inscribe them in their flags, these great words joining liberty and fraternity which make revolutions and undo thrones?

THE KING
(impatiently)
Sir, if the people you are accusing conspire with foreigners, they will be punished severely.

DE GEVRY
Sire, perhaps it would be better to prevent than repress—

THE KING
Prevent? And how?

ARAMIS
By withdrawing from these rebels the guarantees they abuse, by shutting their temples, by confiscating their wealth, by converting them, by force if need be: I mean by putting them to the necessity of abjuring or emigrating.

THE KING
Ah, indeed! Sir, have you thought that what you are proposing to me is nothing less than the revocation of the Edict of Nantes?

ARAMIS
Indeed, Sire, nothing less than that.

THE KING
Think that it was my ancestor, it was Henry IV, it was the great Henry who signed that edict!

ARAMIS
Well, it will be the grandson, it will be Louis XIV, it will be Louis the Great, who rips it up, that's all.

THE KING
(after a pause)
No, no—let's break this off—I will never consent to despoil, to persecute my subjects.

ARAMIS
(aside)
Come! It's no longer necessary to count on the woman!
(aloud)
It suffices! Your Majesty will consider.
(he bows to take his leave)

THE KING
(retaining him)
One moment, sir—that person of whom you were speaking to me just now—

ARAMIS
He's coming back to her.
(aloud and feigning to search)
That person?

THE KING
Yes, that little protégée of Madame Scarron.

ARAMIS
(innocently)
Miss de la Tremblaye?

THE KING
You know her?

ARAMIS
Yes, Sire—Miss de la Tremblaye is from an honest Breton family—who've given their proof of it in the service of the state. She deserves all the attention all the favors with which the King deigns to honor her—I thought that a role, however modest it might be, near Her Majesty, the Queen, could come to the assistance of her modest resources.

THE KING
You're right, sir—we must repair to the daughter the involuntarily prejudice her parents received from our forgetfulness.

Miss de la Tremblaye will be a lady of honor to the Queen.

ARAMIS
Ah, Sire, your benevolence is full of delicacy.

THE KING
But you know the Queen permits me only to recommend to her women in possession of a husband.

ARAMIS
Well, Sire, we will find one for Miss de la Tremblaye.

THE KING
That's it—provide her with one soon. I'll speak to the Queen about our protégée. If you come this evening, for cards, I'll be glad to meet you.

ARAMIS
(bowing)
I will take care not to fail, Sire—

THE KING
You'll be able to hear Her Majesty herself announce the good news to this interesting orphan—au revoir, my dear Duke, au revoir.

MAUPERTIUS
Open the gates.
(the King leaves by the left)

(The court returns and follows the King out of the left. The crowd stretches behind him uttering exclamations. Aramis moves apart on the arm of Boislaurier who has reentered.)

BOISLAURIER
So, His Majesty called you, my dear Duke?

ARAMIS
Yes, my old friend! Gambling has brought us back. Game played, game won!

(They disappear in conversation.)

(Two Musketeers are on guard duty on the terrace Joel and Petit Renaud have entered from the right on a wave of people. They've watched the procession slip off. They come forward.)

JOEL
By jimminy! How fine this court is!

PETIT RENAUD
And how willingly the good people of France forget that. They are wearing worn out breeches and a vest out at the elbows, while admiring the gilded dress, the lace and feathers of the sovereign and great lords!

JOEL
It suffices, my comrade! We didn't come here to philosophize. Let's try to put our hand on the character I need.

(Brigadier Brégy with two musketeers arrives by the left and relieves the functionaries at the back.)

PETIT RENAUD
That blue cassock and those crosses on the breast which Bonlarron spoke to us about.

JOEL
Yes—they are musketeers and the one who commands them really seems to me to have aged in harness.

PETIT RENAUD
He's old enough to give us information!
(Brégy raises his voice)
But he doesn't seem easy going.

(Brégy, who has replaced the two musketeers starts to march off with his men and heads toward the right.)

JOEL
(stopping Brégy)
Excuse me, sir.

BRÉGY
(scrutinizing him)
What do you want with me, young cock?

PETIT RENAUD
(proudly)
We are both cocks?

JOEL
Is it permitted for me to ask you if you belong to the illustrious company of musketeers?

BRÉGY
(shrugging)
Damn! At least you don't take us for Swiss guards.

JOEL
In that case, you would have had knowledge of a certain D'Artagnan?

BRÉGY
Mr. D'Artagnan? Our former Captain! Why are you asking me if I knew Mr. D'Artagnan? Is it because I'm in the corps for 30 years without having gotten anything but the grade of Brigadier?

JOEL
Oh! Sir, you cannot think that!

BRÉGY
Call me right away—old cassock!

PETIT RENAUD
We wouldn't dare, sir!

JOEL
But you said: Our former captain—Mr. D'Artagnan is no longer in service?

BRÉGY
Hey! Now there's the news he's been dead a long while! Killed in the campaign in Friesland by a ball from a cannon which crushed his chest.

JOEL
(to himself, with regret)
Dead!
(to Brégy)
Yet another word, please. Has one of the three names I am going to mention ever struck your ear! Athos, Aramis, Porthos?

BRÉGY
Athos! Aramis! Porthos! Yes, by jove! I recall those names, and those who bore them! Athos, a great lord from I don't know what country—who dazzled us with his sovereign mien and his magnificent manners!

JOEL
And the others, I beg you, the others?

BRÉGY
Aramis, a priest disguised as a musketeer.

JOEL
And the other, sir, the other?

BRÉGY
Porthos! A glutton, a brute, and a braggart!

JOEL
Sir!

BRÉGY
And dumb! Oh, very dumb!

JOEL
(with controlled rage)
Plague—you are not charitable to your former companions in arms.

BRÉGY
Oh! That's because they had so much luck, they did! Whereas I—! Reduced to vegetating as a subaltern to tighten my belt to give daily bread to my passions.

JOEL
Finally, this Aramis? This Porthos?

BRÉGY
One was made a priest, the other baron! Royal favors that they hastened to return with ingratitude.

JOEL
(between his teeth)
You are saying?

BRÉGY
I am saying that the priest from Vannes and the Baron from Vallon immersed themselves in the plot which led to the arrest of Fouquet! I say it was they who were defending Belle Isle against the King's men—and the result of this brawl they disappeared from the corps! I say finally, that I saw the judgment that

condémned the two accomplices for the crime of High Treason!

JOEL
(exploding)
Porthos, a traitor! You lie!

BRÉGY
Me!

(He's going to rush Joel; the musketeers throw themselves between them. The Brigadier moves them away with a gesture, then he strides towards the young man and looks at him frowningly.)

BRÉGY
Young man, you've just said a word.

JOEL
(coldly)
I was not aware to what it obliged me, and I am at your orders, sir.

BRÉGY
Right here, on the sport, we are going to dance a rondo to the tune of clashing blades.

PETIT RENAUD
If it's a question of dancing and music I am joining the quadrille.

D'ESPERON
Eh, sir! Your comrade has been warming our ears too long! I wouldn't be annoyed to make him feel it, were it only by proxy.

PETIT RENAUD
At your orders!

DE GEVRY
(and another musketeer, interposing)
Gentlemen, gentlemen!

DE CHAMPVALLIER
To draw your sword in a royal residence.

BRÉGY
Fine! All these dandies of the court have accompanied the King into the forest.

D'ESPERON
No one will disturb us.

PETIT RENAUD
Besides, it won't take long—!

JOEL
We will commence whenever your please.

BRÉGY
(to his companions)
Gentlemen, let two of you serve as witnesses, and the others stand watch!
(to the two who remain)
You won't meddle in what is going on other than to witness at need that things have taken place in a decent manner—and that we have dealt with these gentlemen according to the rules.

PETIT RENAUD
He speaks if it were already done!

JOEL
(to Brégy)
I am yours, sir.

(The go "on guard". Petit Renaud and Esperon do so as well.)

JOEL
Combat!

PETIT RENAUD
(to Esperon)
You have no recommendation in extremis to address to these gentlemen?

D'ESPERON
Braggart.

BRÉGY
(pushing Joel)
Take care of yourself, kid.

JOEL
(parrying)
I will try, my veteran.

D'ESPERON
(to Petit Renaud with whom he has not been slow to be engaged body to body)
You are a Gascon, sir?

PETIT RENAUD
Like Henry IV, God's blood!

D'ESPERON
I feel your steel!

BRÉGY
(who's been hurt)
Oh! Oh! The cadet has done wrong! And here I wanted to protect him—to give him a simple scratch—now I am obliged

to kill him.

D'ESPERON
(as he duels)
So it's in the honor of Mr. Porthos we are fighting.

PETIT RENAUD
That's the way it seems to me.

D'ESPERON
And why?

BRÉGY
(struck dead)
Ah!

JOEL
(stopping, to D'Esperon)
Why? Because he was my father!

(The Musketeers press around Brégy; Petit Renaud and D'Esperon disappear for an instant into the trees—Joel doesn't budge and calmly puts his sword in its scabbard.)

(Enter De Maupertius and guards.)

DE MAUPERTIUS
A duel? Scoffing at the edicts! Who killed this gentleman?

JOEL
Me!

(The musketeers raise Brégy's body.)

DE MAUPERTIUS
I arrest you in the name of the King.

(The Guards arrest Joel.)

CURTAIN

ACT II
SCENE IV

In the Bastille.

The interior of the mid-size cell. To the right a bunk, above it a barred window, to the left a door, and a stool. Pierre Lesage is standing on his bunk to finish putting a final touch to the bars on his window. He interrupts his work to listen.

LeSAGE
Someone's coming.
(he hides his file and lets himself slide down onto his bunk where he feigns sleep. Noise of bolts—the door opens)

JAILOR
(to Joel)
Enter! Here's your lodging.

LeSAGE
(feigning to wake up)
What's going on?

JAILOR
I'm bringing you a temporary companion—tomorrow morning you will give him this cell. You will be installed elsewhere.

LeSAGE
(terrified)
Ah!

JOEL
(emerging from his stupor, to Jailor)
Sir, a word, I beg you—

JAILOR
Make it fast!

JOEL
I would be grateful to be informed in what place I am for the moment.

JAILOR
Wise guy! As if you didn't know as well as I, you are in the Bastille.
(He leaves and bolts the door.)

JOEL
In the Bastille! I am in the Bastille!
(he remains as if annihilated on the stool)

LeSAGE
(in his bed, looking at Joel angrily)
Oh! This man who's coming strikes my labor into impotence! A spy, perhaps.
(raising his voice)
Sir?

JOEL
(distractedly)
Sir!

LeSAGE
(getting out of bed)
Do I dare ask why you are a prisoner?

JOEL
Because I crossed swords with a musketeer of the King.

LeSAGE
Sonofabitch! Your case is serious. His Majesty doesn't play with duelists. You're a gentleman, no doubt.

JOEL
I think so—but I have only my conviction to prove it.

LeSAGE
In that case, you will not be decapitated. Only it is probable that you will be hanged!

JOEL
Hanged! The Devil—that would bore me. Down there, in my country, I saw a Norman hanged, an honest horse jobber who found the rope a little bit harder for having stolen a halter. It's true the horse was at the end of its tether. Yuck—what a villainous death that was. I am still shivering form it—brrr!

LeSAGE
(looking him over)
The accent of frankness! This lad won't betray me!
(mysteriously)
Well—this hideous death it's up to you get yourself out of it!

JOEL
How's that.

LeSAGE
By accompanying me, soon!

JOEL
Huh?

LeSAGE
I expect to escape tonight.

JOEL
You're escaping? Then it's possible to get out of the Bastille?

LeSAGE
Yes—if you work, as I did, from the time one's taken captive to prepare for your flight. See, with this old knife, I've manufactured this file. With the wool from my bed covers I've made this rope.
(he pulls out objects from under the beam of the bed, which he points to)
With my file—I have patiently sawed through two bars of this window. These two bars are held up only by a bit of iron.
(he gives a last tap to the file)
There—they are detached!

JOEL
Thanks! I won't even attempt it.

LeSAGE
I understand! Danger terrifies you!

JOEL
You don't understand at all! Only, to flee, would be to admit I am guilty. So, when there's nothing to be reproached for, one is not afraid of confronting justice.

LeSAGE
(abruptly)
At your ease. But you are not, at least, going to prevent me from accomplishing

what I have decided? You are not going to call, to warn the jailor?

JOEL
Ah, indeed! What do you take me for?

LeSAGE
Pardon! Ah! Pardon. Misfortune makes you cautious.

JOEL
Act as seems good to you—I hear nothing, I see nothing!
(turning and offering him his hand)
Goodbye and good luck!

LeSAGE
You are offering your hand to me? Ah, if you knew who I am!

JOEL
(gravely)
I know that you are a man in danger of death and I am going to pray God to assist you.

LeSAGE
(emotionally)
Thanks! It's been a long while since I've shaken the hand of an honest men. May this grasp bring me good luck!
(with determination)
And now to work!
(he clambers up on his bunk and hoists himself to the window, looking at Joel)

LeSAGE
He's much happier than I am!
He can pray.
(he leans on the opening)
Let's go—with the grace of God.

(he descends outside and disappears)

JOEL
(alone)
Free! I could have been! To run to the home of this good Madame Scarron—to see Aurora.
(listening)
Oh—that wind which howls against the walls! Despite myself, I cannot prevent myself from trembling for the poor devil who just adventured into this storm, at the end of a rope!
(a shot)
Ah! The wretch—they saw him. Did they hit him?
(after a silence)
That's odd—his face doesn't come back to me exactly. And yet when I think of the peril he's running at this moment, I want to murmur the prayer that our Breton women recite on stormy nights for sailors lost at sea.
(he prays silently)

VOICE OF THE JAILOR
(in the wings)
This way! This way!

(The Jailor enters with two soldiers carrying Pierre Lesage mortally wounded.)

JAILOR
(pointing to the bed)
Place him there.
(noticing Joel)
Heavens! The other one didn't budge—run wake up the major—you—inform the doctor.

LeSAGE
Useless! It's not a doctor, it's a priest I need.

JAILOR
A priest.

JOEL
One doesn't refuse a priest to a dying man.

JAILOR
So be it! I warn you there's an eye on this window and on this door.
(he leaves)

LeSAGE
Water! I'm thirsty.

JOEL
(giving him a jug)
Here!

LeSAGE
Thanks—
(with a shiver)
My God!
I'm suffocating.
(Joel supports him)
(taking the hand from his wound, Lesage touches a medallion hanging from his neck)
Oh! This letter that reminds me of all I wish to forget! Here! Take it! Keep it!
(he pulls off the medallion)

JOEL
What?

LeSAGE
Keep it, I tell you! In this letter, Madame de Montespan asked—a wretch for a poison with which to rid herself of a rival.

JOEL
(taking the letter)
What do you want me to do with this letter?

LeSAGE
Take it, I tell you! Your hand, one more time, your hand! May it bring me the pardon I am awaiting before dying!
(he expires)

(The Major, the doctor, soldiers, and guards appear.)

JOEL
(to doctor)
Come, sir—in the name of heaven, come quickly!

DOCTOR
(after having examined LeSage)
Dead!

(Joel bows, the others present uncover except for the Jailor.)

JOEL
(to Jailor)
Didn't you hear?

JAILOR
(brutally)
Right! He's dead!

JOEL
(tearing the jailor's hat off and throwing it on the ground)
Well—before the dead, one takes off one's hat.

MAJOR
Two bars broken. Take this prisoner to another cell.
(to doctor)

You will take care to write that Number 141 died of a gunshot in an attempt to escape.

DOCTOR
And this number 141 was—?

MAJOR
Pierre Lesage, poisoner.

JOEL
Oh!

(He leaves with the Jailor.)

CURTAIN

ACT II
SCENE V

The Queen's Cards.

(A gallery of the Chateau giving on several rooms. At back, the card room. To the left, apartments belonging to the King. Musketeers at the exterior doors. Pages at the doors of the apartments.)

FRANÇOISE
(to Aurora)
No, my child, don't try to protest. You don't yet know how to lie. Here now, why this emotion when I question you like an older sister? Do you have to tremble like that to admit you are in love.

AURORA
Eh! What, you've guessed?

FRANÇOISE
Without any sorcery. Your candid soul is reflected in your features.
(observing her)
Anyway, could it be otherwise in a court populated with gallant cavaliers and when, in the eyes of all the ladies, the King passes for the most handsome, the noblest gentleman in his kingdom.

AURORA
The King! Why I haven't even looked at him! Oh! It's not the King that I love, Madame?

FRANÇOISE
Then who? Mr. Joel, perhaps.
(Aurora lowers her eyes)
Come on—where's my wit? To suspect this child? No!
(aloud)
You see, the sly-boots?
Hey, why it's nothing to blush about, on the contrary! Love him and with all your soul—this brave lad, so proud, so honest, so different from these handsome gentlemen for whom love is only a pleasant whim, and women only a conceited fantasy.

AURORA
(taking her hand)
Oh! How good you are, Madame!

PAGE
(from the right, announcing)
The King!
(conversation amongst the groups)

AURORA
(frightened despite herself)
The King!

THE KING
(entering with Louvois)
May I not be a trouble to the party, ladies! And let no one be disturbed. I desire it! I wish it!
(bowing before Aurora while Louvois goes to mix in with the groups)
Do I have, Miss, the misfortune, that my presence is an object of terror to you?

AURORA
Oh! Sire, please attribute it only to astonishment, to respect—I am confused that Your Majesty notices it—

THE KING
Confused! And why, I beg you? What would render me confused would be for the King of France to hesitate to excuse himself for having, whatever may be the cause, placed emotion in such a charming face!

PAGE
(at the left, announcing)
The Queen!

(The Queen emerges from her apartments. At a glance from Louis, Mme de Montespan detaches herself from a group and goes toward the Queen.)

MME de MONTESPAN
(with humility after a deep curtsy)
Your Majesty will permit me to submit to her the decision I've reached to leave the court and retire to my domain in Clagny—if the Queen will deign to consent to it?

THE QUEEN
(haughtily)
Madame, I haven't the right to oppose your plans! It's up to the King to retain you or authorize your retreat. His Majesty, whom you must have consulted before me, has doubtless made you aware of his will. Whatever he's done will be fine!
(Mme de Montespan bows and prepares to withdraw—then stops as the Queen addresses the King)
Sire, you spoke to me of a young girl you wanted to present to me?

THE KING
(making Aurora came forward)
Here's Miss de la Tremblaye, Madame!

THE QUEEN
Miss, I want you to become part of our house—

AURORA
Oh! Madame—!

THE QUEEN
(with kindness)
Pull yourself together, child. They told me that your father died almost without money, after having long and bravely served the State. What I am granting you here, with the consent of the King, is not a favor as you seem to believe. It's the beginning of reparations!

THE KING
So you see, Miss, we are already greatly occupied with you. Yes, we have decided that you will be dowered, after a brief delay, so that a spouse worthy of such a fortune—

AURORA
(with terror)
Sire!

THE KING
Custom demands it for persons attached to the service of Her Majesty.
(he leaves followed by part of the court)

THE QUEEN
Miss de la Tremblaye will take possession of her duties the day after the day she has presented her husband to us.

AURORA
(aside)
Oh! My God!

FRANÇOISE
(to Aurora)
Control yourself, you must!
(to the Queen, bowing)
Miss de la Tremblaye, knows only how deeply touched she must be by the favors of the Queen.

(The Queen, followed by the rest of the court, goes into the game room at the back.)

AURORA
(after the exodus throws herself weeping into Françoise' arms)
Ah! Madame—Madame!

MME de MONTESPAN
(who remained at the side, comes forward—with irony)
I am happy to meet Miss de la Tremblaye and to present her my compliments on her approaching marriage and her recent fortune.

FRANÇOISE
(drily)
You were listening, Madame?

MME de MONTESPAN
Excuse me, I heard, which is quite different.
(to Aurora, still with irony)
Yes, Miss, yes, I know that the King wishes you well! That's why I am coming humbly to place myself under all powerful protection.

AURORA
My protection—?

MME de MONTESPAN
Intercede with His Majesty so he will permit me to return to the court—oh! As a spectator, as disinterested. There are so many curious things for folks with nothing more to do to see there!

AURORA
(troubled)
Why, Madame—

MME de MONTESPAN
Intercede for me, Miss, and I am sure of it, all power will give way before yours—Don't you have youth which conquers and charms? Without counting on virtue which is no question, not the least of your graces.

AURORA
(very upset)
My God, under what title would I have the power you attribute to me?

MME de MONTESPAN
Under what title? You ask me under what title? You are very modest, my sweet.

FRANÇOISE
(to the Marquise)
On my salvation, Madame, you're wrong to suspect and to accuse—?

(The King has just entered and stops.)

AURORA
(distracted)
Why of what am I accused?

MME de MONTESPAN
Why of aspiring to—

THE KING
(to Mme de Montespan)
Enough! Not another word!
(to Françoise)
Take Miss de la Tremblaye away, Madame!

(Françoise and Aurora leave.)

(The King instinctively follows Aurora with his eyes.)

MME de MONTESPAN
(who has observed him)
Well, Sire—!

THE KING
(seeing his glance discovered)
Well, Madame—you are not mistaken!

MME de MONTESPAN
(exploding)
You admit it! Then let her tremble!

THE KING
You're the one who should tremble! After a long time, you have exhausted my patience. I forbid you to return to Saint Germain!

MME de MONTESPAN
You forbid me?

THE KING
If you dare to reappear here—I swear to God—

MME de MONTESPAN
Perhaps you'll have me arrested? And where to take me? To the Bastille, like Lauzun of whom you were jealous? To Pignerol, like Fouquet who was LaVallière's lover prior to you?

THE KING
Madame!

MME de MONTESPAN
(continuing)
To the Island of Sainte-Marguerite, with a mask of steel like that mysterious prisoner?

THE KING
No, Madame, not to the Bastille, not to Pignerol, not to the Isle of Saint Marguerite! But to the Grand Chalet where poisoners are condémned and to la Grève where they are executed.

(Mme de Montespan remains speechless for a moment. Calm, the King, seeing some young gentlemen enter, among them Louvois opens a side door into his apartments, and indicating it to Mme de Montespan.)

THE KING
Here, Madame, your face bears traces of emotion which must not be perceived—this way, you can leave the chateau without being seen.
(she starts to leave and as she passes by him)
Remember the death of Miss Fontange!

MME de MONTESPAN
(leaving and raising her head)
I'll recall it, Sire!

(she leaves)

THE KING
(to Louvois)
Come closer, Mr. Louvois, you told me just now that Duke Charles of Lorraine has just fought his way into Freibourg, from which he is threatening our situation in the east.

LOUVOIS
Yes, Sire, and I was going to add that unhappily our garrisons are completely insufficient.

THE KING
Can't they be reinforced?

LOUVOIS
Surely, but I was hesitating to do it.

THE KING
What! Explain yourself—!

LOUVOIS
Sire, the circumstances advise us to observe an extreme reserve. To draw the sword, when, by a common agreement the whole world seems to have put it back in the scabbard.

THE KING
Indeed, sir, indeed.

LOUVOIS
Eh! My God, let's let Prince Charles make big eyes at us from Freibourg. If he attacks us, we will receive him. But let's beware going to seek him across the Rhine with the river behind us to cut off any retreat.

(Françoise is in a group of ladies, near Aurora—at the minister's words. She makes a gesture which the King notices.)

THE KING
(to Françoise)
Madame, the Duke of Maine, your pupil, recently told me you were of precisely the same opinion. Prove it to us, by lending us the support of your knowledge. You heard, Mr. Louvois?

FRANÇOISE
Oh! Most involuntarily, Sire.

THE KING
And you share his ideas?

FRANÇOISE
(after a pause)
No, Sire!

THE KING
Ah! Really, and why? Speak frankly—

FRANÇOISE
Well, since Your Majesty authorizes me to give my opinion on a subject quite beyond the province of my sex, I dare to declare, in all humility, that energetic action seems to me more suited to hasten the rupture of the course of negotiations. For too long a time, Duke Charles has braved the might of our arms! Let's interrupt his plans against the walls of Freibourg! The Rhine will be behind us to cut off retreat? So much the better! We have no wish to retreat that I know of. I know our French—they will go forward—for they prefer fire to water.

THE KING
Now there's the language of a French woman devoted to king and country!

LOUVOIS
What does Your Majesty decide?

THE KING
Tomorrow morning I will give you my instructions for Marshal Créqui.
(Louvois bows and leaves—to Françoise)
Thanks, Madame. Truly, they were not wrong to bestow on you the surname, "Madame Wisdom."

FRANÇOISE
I don't deserve it, Sire—I am only a devoted subject who, in dedicating herself to the education of your children is accustomed to love through them, the glory of the King.

THE KING
Madame, continue to protect them, those children, the treasures of your mind and heart. The King of France will undertake to acquit himself of the debts of the Father.
(to Aurora)
And you, Miss, are you satisfied?

FRANÇOISE
Ah, Sire, how could she fail to be?

THE KING
It's not I you must thank—it's your friends. Madame Scarron, first of all and then Mr. D'Alaméda.

AURORA
Mr. de Alaméda?

THE KING
(to Aramis who appears among the courtiers)
Come, Mr. Duke, and admire your wish.

AURORA
The Chevalier d'Herbaly!

ARAMIS
The Duke of Alaméda!

THE KING
We are going to give you leisure to renew the acquaintance.

(He goes off with all the court into the game room. The curtains of the first room close.)

AURORA
Eh! What, it's to you I owe all this?

ARAMIS
You owe nothing, except to yourself, and I will prove it to you if you give me a few moment's audience.

AURORA
An audience? Now? Here?

ARAMIS
Everybody is at the Queen's gaming—

AURORA
I am at your orders, Duke—

ARAMIS
If you were lost in the depths of your province, you were not unaware of what role Louise de la Vallière, the first inclination of our changeable sovereign was used to playing this court. You can no longer be unaware of what role the Marquise de Montespan played here until yesterday.

AURORA
It's true they told me the adventure of the first and how she cruelly expiates to this very hour the sin of being unable to resist her heart.

As for the second, all I know of her is that she's leaving Saint Germain.

ARAMIS
Do you know also that the King is smitten by a new person?

AURORA
A new person?

ARAMIS
Louis, disabused of Mme de Montespan, is madly taken by another person, an adorable creature who—if she is pliable to the advise of a friend—being well brought up, would never have to fear of being entombed, like her predecessor, and who, alone, will have this envied glory of fixing under her sway the most powerful of monarchs, the most capricious because the most faithful of lovers.

AURORA
Duke, you must be a bit indulgent; I am only a poor provincial girl—and I ask myself truly—

ARAMIS
What! You have not grasped that this adorable and adored creature—is you!

AURORA
My God, my God!
(rising)

ARAMIS
Calm down, child, calm down! If you were a vulgar woman, I would show you a whole court prostrated at your feet in dazzling festivities, the concert of praise. But you are as good as you are beautiful and I will say to you simply the people who have cursed the name of favorites who preceded you will learn to bless yours!

(Aurora passes silently before Aramis and curtsies to him as if to withdraw.)

ARAMIS
Well! What are you doing? Where are you going?

AURORA
I am leaving the chateau, sir—I am leaving the court, and returning to my poor Breton village whose peasants have not yet forgotten to respect the daughter of their former Lord.

ARAMIS
Leave? Why that's madness!

AURORA
Ah! I have the firm conviction that you didn't intend to offend me! I was alone—without resource. You were offering me means of becoming rich and powerful. It's a great kindness on your part and it's I who am asking your pardon for being unable to make use of it.

ARAMIS
Miss—

AURORA
Goodbye, sir—we will never see each other any more. Down there where I will live in isolation and prayer, I promise you to recollect only our first meeting.

(She takes a few steps to leave then stops to lean on the back of a chair as if ill.)

ARAMIS
(aside)
Ah! Ah! I was on the wrong path. I've got to keep her.
(after a moment's consideration going to Aurora)
Oh, my child, my dear child how happy you are making me!

AURORA
Happy!

ARAMIS
And when I think I was on the point of suspecting you. Yes, I doubted you, I confess it—one moment—oh—merely for a moment. I was afraid of seeing you succumb to this test.

AURORA
A test! It was a test!

ARAMIS
Why nothing else.

AURORA
Ah, sir! You made me suffer cruelly.

ARAMIS
Yes, once more: Pardon!

AURORA
But what was the good of this test?

ARAMIS
(aside)
The Devil.

AURORA
Why did you give yourself so much trouble to cause me so much ill?

ARAMIS
(aside)
Come on, I'm not allowed to be caught napping.
(aloud)
What you don't grasp it?
(negative gesture by Aurora)
Well, suppose that someone, that a friend, had begged me, had charged me with assuring myself clearly—that you were not sacrificing to an un-hoped for fate—the tenderness of a man sincerely smitten—

AURORA
(excitedly)
Ah! Joel—right?

ARAMIS
(momentarily surprised)
Joel? Yes, Joel! Effectively, he loves you—but he has scruples which do him honor, "I would die of sorrow", he said to me this morning, "If later she came to pity the humility of my situation."

AURORA
Is it possible he judged me so ill?

ARAMIS
That's when the idea came to me of playing with you the role of Satan to Eve. Thanks to heaven the trial succeeded to the inclination of our wishes. You despised a throne to keep the man, you've chosen. That's fine! That's very fine!

AURORA
What's he doing? What more did he say to you? Is he still thinking of me the way I am of him?

(Aramis, places of finger on his lips, smiling, indicating to Aurora the court entering with the King who is chatting with Manpertius.)

AURORA
(confused, seeks refuge with Françoise)
Oh, pardon, sir!
(to Françoise)
Come, Madame, come—!

(They vanish into another salon.)

ARAMIS
(aside)
Ah! Women! It's rightly said they are capable of anything—even goodness! Meanwhile, to keep this little girl at court, I must find this Joel again.

(The doorkeepers are relieved and light salons at the back full of lords and ladies.)

THE KING
What are you telling me, sir? A duel under my window! Now that's imprudent—Indeed I think—that the culprits are at this moment already in the hands of justice.

DE MAUPERTIUS
The survivor's been arrested, Sire—for there was a dead man in the person of Brigadier Brégy!

THE KING
One of my musketeers! And the one who struck him down—

who is he?

DE MAUPERTIUS
A young man! A sort of peasant—a Breton.

ARAMIS
(raising his head)
A Breton!

DE MAUPERTIUS
Who's wearing the costume of the people of Belle Isle-en-mer.

ARAMIS
(aside)
Oh, great!

DE MAUPERTIUS
He told me his name's Joel.

THE KING
Joel.

ARAMIS
(aside)
Well, he didn't lose any time!

THE KING
Where will it end if rustics take up swords against our gentlemen? And what's been done with this clown?

DE MAUPERTIUS
I had him sent to the Bastille, while awaiting Your Majesty's orders—

THE KING
Fine.

(Maupertius distances himself.)

ARAMIS
(coming forward)
Oh! Sire, it's been a long time that it's been said that clemency is the finest virtue of kings, as the right of grace their most beautiful attribute.

THE KING
On my soul, Duke, I like to believe that you are not going to intercede on behalf of this ruffian?

ARAMIS
I shall still have that audacity, Sire!

THE KING
Sir, this Joel is a great culprit!

ARAMIS
In that case, it's the King's generosity that I am addressing myself, not to his justice.

THE KING
Yet once more—what are you thinking of? A man who braves our edicts? Who has killed, one of our servants—and who doesn't even have the excuse of belonging to our nobility? You know him? He's so dear to you?

ARAMIS
Dear to me? Not the least in the world? I've hardly seen him once in my life!

THE KING
Well?

ARAMIS
Well—he is useful to us! Which is of more importance—

THE KING
Useful? And what would you make of him?

ARAMIS
The husband of Miss de la Tremblaye!

THE KING
What do you mean?

ARAMIS
(bowing)
He loves her, Sire.

THE KING
And Miss de la Tremblaye?

ARAMIS
I affirm to Your Majesty that she loves no one!

THE KING
Duke, you are right! This man shall live! This man will be the husband of Miss de la Tremblaye!

CURTAIN

ACT III
SCENE VI

The Diplomacy of Aramis.

A small salon richly decorated with a main door and large windows—side doors to the left, a table.

A Sergeant with four guards and Joel.

SERGEANT
(to Bazin)
Here's the prisoner I am directed to deliver to you.

BAZIN
Very good! You may withdraw.

(Exit of Sergeant and guards.)

JOEL
(looking around)
Ah, indeed! Where the devil am I?

ARAMIS
(entering)
You are at my home, my dear gentleman!

JOEL
The old lord from the Inn of the Golden Heron!

ARAMIS
Yes, I am the Duke of Alaméda, Ambassador of His Catholic Majesty.

JOEL
The Duke of Alaméda? Ambassador of His Catholic Majesty? Doggone! I don't get it at all.

ARAMIS
So I'm going to explain to you? Bazin—a seat for the Chevalier.

JOEL
(to himself)
Why the devil is he calling me, Chevalier?

ARAMIS
(be seated. You are here in my little residence at Saint Germain, which will be yours until new orders. The garden through which you came in gives on the forest, but from this side, it's the town and the chateau's chapel can be observed from the window.

JOEL
And there I was, thinking they were going to take me before my judges when they came to remove me from the Bastille this morning—for I was in the Bastille—

ARAMIS
Yes, I know—for a sword blow—unfortunately well enough delivered—ah, you are a matador! The champion of Belle Isle! But the King having signed the order for your release—

JOEL
His Majesty signed the order?

ARAMIS
He signed the order—

JOEL
He's pardoning me—?

ARAMIS
Fully and completely.

JOEL
And they won't try me?

ARAMIS
Not the least in the world—

JOEL
They're not going to condémn me?

ARAMIS
Not any longer—

JOEL
(with ah significant gesture)
They aren't—

ARAMIS
Don't worry. Your head is henceforth solidly on your shoulders. And truly, it would have been a shame to touch it because it is very good right where it is.

JOEL
Doggone it! Long live the King in that case! And long live you, too, Mr. Ambassador of His Catholic Majesty! For you interceded for me, I am certain of it. Yes, it's to you I owe being free! And if ever you have need of my arm, of my blood, of my life.

ARAMIS
Hey, my boy, are you quite sure all that actually belongs to you?

JOEL
Damn!

ARAMIS
Haven't you already disposed of all that?

JOEL
Deposed! To whom?

ARAMIS
To the woman you love!

JOEL
(aside)
Aurora! It's true—I was forgetting Aurora.
(aloud)
Sir, you've shown me the concern of a father. I will preserve for you the gratitude of a son. But from one hour to the next it will have no bounds if you will grant me the leave I need without delay so I can run to deal with my affairs.

ARAMIS
Are you thinking of it, scatterbrain that you are? And the ceremony that must take place in a few moments.

JOEL
Ceremony! What ceremony?

ARAMIS
You've hardly got time to dress properly as the occasion demands.

JOEL
Dress properly?

FIRST LACKEY
(entering)
The tailor of Mr. Chevalier.

SECOND LACKEY
The hairdresser of Mr. Chevalier.

THIRD LACKEY
The valet of Mr. Chevalier.

(The tradesmen enter after the lackeys and arrange themselves at the back.)

ARAMIS
(to Joel)
Wait, here's a bunch of artists directed expressly to bring about your metamorphosis.

JOEL
A valet, a hairdresser, a tailor?

ARAMIS
Let yourself do it, my young friend. We have only your good in sight. We will prove it to you soon.

JOEL
Why, it's not possible. I—

ARAMIS
Ah! Now then, are you rebelling already against the one you call your savior?

JOEL
Still—

ARAMIS
(pushing him in a friendly way toward the right)
Then go and prepare yourself, Chevalier—and return quickly, we still have a lot to discuss.

JOEL
Let's go, I'm letting myself do it—

(He leaves.)

ARAMIS
And you, gentlemen, I am confiding a savage to you—try to return him to me as a man with a fine manner—

(The valet, the hairdresser and the tailor leave with lackeys.)

ARAMIS
Now see where you've got to, Aramis! Ah! D'Artagnan, Athos, Porthos, my valiant friends! If you could see into what a wretched spider web I am striving to weave at this moment your shoulders would shrug with compassion and disdain! You, the valiant champions of former struggles—struggles where we fought the good fight for oppressed queens or kings without crowns! Ah! times have changed. Today the great adventures in which we risked losing our heads on the block with the Montmorency and Cing Mars have given way to parlor intrigues—sad chess board, where this hand which was once powerful enough to shake a throne, is reduced like that of pawns to move the marionettes of the court.

BAZIN
The man Your Excellency is expecting has just arrived.

ARAMIS
Bring him in—let's not let Miss de la Tremblaye cause us to forget Freibourg! The taking of that town by Mr. de Créqui would be the evident proof of the impotence of Mr. de Lorraine, the secret ally of my master! The place must be held at least until the end of negotiations at Niemiegen. A French victory would render the King of France more intractable by increasing his prestige and his pride!

BAZIN
(introducing Asdrubal)
(aside)
The villainous folks with whom we practice politics.
(aloud)
Enter! Here is Milord.

ASDRUBAL
(bowing)
Excellency.

ARAMIS
Come closer and open your ears.

ASDRUBAL
I am listening, Milord.

ARAMIS
And shut your mouth.

ASDRUBAL
I am mute!

ARAMIS
Yesterday evening, returning to the Chateau, I reached my hotel on foot—in the company of Mr. Boislaurier—it was around 11 o'clock.

ASDRUBAL
Eleven o'clock? What could I have been doing at that hour? I was sleeping the sleep of the just.

ARAMIS
You believe that?

ASDRUBAL
I am sure of it, Milord.

ARAMIS
And as for me, I am sure of the contrary.

ASDRUBAL
Ah! Your Excellency is—

ARAMIS
Certain that you were not sleeping at 11 o'clock.

ASDRUBAL
Damnation! If Your Excellency is certain, indeed perhaps.

ARAMIS
I told you to keep your ears peeled.

ASDRUBAL
And my mouth shut! I am mute!

ARAMIS
A downpour forced Mr. Boislaurier and myself to seek shelter in one of the woodcutter's cabins which adjoin the forest. The one in which we were refuged had two rooms. We would have stopped in the first, Boislaurer having noticed, with his trained flair, that there was someone in the second.

ASDRUBAL
No doubt the woodcutter—

ARAMIS
You think so? It's possible! But another person was with him and was speaking quite low, oh! Very low! The rain wasn't slow to stop and you can imagine that Boislaurier, curiosity makes the man, wanted to know what mysterious strollers we had failed to surprise. He watched their exit—strange event! The pretended woodcutter had airs of a cut-throat! If at that moment you weren't sleeping the sleep of the just, I would have sworn it was you.

ASDRUBAL
Milord is teasing me!

ARAMIS
(drily)
Come now, down with masks—! It was you! Plague, my dear chap, you need the King's marvels. You had a clandestine rendezvous with LaMontespan.

ASDRUBAL
Oh! Love didn't count in this matter.

ARAMIS
Shut up!

ASDRUBAL
I am mute.

ARAMIS
Oh! Master Asdrubal, I know you—You are the last survivor of the accomplices of LaVoisin. At the time of her trial you took a false name and the attributes of a captain which allowed you to give the slip to the police. But in reality you are the brother of

Pierre Lesage.

ASDRUBAL
Oh! As to that, Milord.

ARAMIS
Peace! Do you know by the way, that your brother is dead?

ASDRUBAL
Dead!

ARAMIS
From a gunshots as he attempted to escape the Bastille.

ASDRUBAL
My poor brother! Our father died of hanging—him, he died of a bullet! Well, that's progress! My poor brother—

ARAMIS
If that death affects you—it is made to rejoice La Montespan. You can tell her at least that Pierre Lesage died without speaking and that nothing was found on his body.

ASDRUBAL
He didn't talk! Ah! What a fine nature! May God care for his soul!

ARAMIS
While waiting, today you alone are in possession of the recipe for that liqueur a few drops of which were poured by your late brother in a cup of milk for Miss de Fontange.

ASDRUBAL
Poor young lady.

ARAMIS
That memory saddens you—let's not dwell on it—and give me right away the flask of the aforesaid liqueur that you promised last night to Mme de Montespan—You hesitate—listen to me—I have only to ring this bell for them to immediately seize from you and this flask that your hand tries to hide. Once taken you will be dragged before Mr. LaReynie, president of the Red Chamber—if I don't call, it's because, satisfied with your attitude I've taken you into my service.

ASDRUBAL
In the service of Your Excellency?

ARAMIS
Yes, I need a servant capable of fulfilling certain delicate and perilous missions—and I need a man with a doubtful past to place himself in my devotion.

ASDRUBAL
A doubtful—past?
(timidly)
Then I think I am able to do the job of Your Excellency.

ARAMIS
Then choose! You will be this man or you will go in the Bastille, in your brother's place, for them to relight LaVoisin's stake.

ASDRUBAL
(proudly)
Milord, I am not afraid of death! But I prefer life! I am yours completely! My brother and Madame LaVoisin have turned out very badly. I hope to smell neither musty nor burned.

ARAMIS
The flask first of all!

ASDRUBAL
Here it is! I will only allow myself to observe to Your Excellency that I promised—

ARAMIS
You mean you were promised an honest reward.

ASDRUBAL
Honest! Oh! Strictly speaking it's all the same to me.

ARAMIS
Well, you shall pocket the reward in exchange for this other flask—
(pulls it from his pocket)
which you will deliver to your client as if it were the one you were asked for.

ASDRUBAL
This other flask?

ARAMIS
Don't worry—it contains only a harmless narcotic.

ASDRUBAL
But if Mme de Montespan notices the fraud?

ARAMIS
By the time she notices it, you will be far from her wrath—I'm coming to the mission I wish to entrust you with. Listen to me. French troops have taken up the siege of Freibourg. Now then, I have great interest in the governor who commands the place. Will you undertake to get yourself in there?

ASDRUBAL
I will get myself in there, Excellency.

ARAMIS
You will cross the siege lines?

ASDRUBAL
Child's play.

ARAMIS
And then?

ASDRUBAL
That's my concern! My interests answers to you for my zeal. Count on me. I've got an inventive mind and once I've decided to do something, the devil—who's a bit my concern—is always my accomplice!

ARAMIS
(delivering a paper to him)
Fine! Take this paper—deliver into the Governor of Freibourg's own hands—for your safety—avoid being seen by the eyes of Mr. de Créqui's French.

(Joel appears at the door on the left in the costume of an officer of a Bombardiers. Seeing a stranger, he moves behind the hanging.)

ASDRUBAL
Have no fear—I have a certain hiding place, and I defy the most nasty to discover the secret.
(he unscrews the pommel of his cane and places the letter in it)
You see, Milord, no more letter. Vanished—and then who suspects the cane of an old man? For I excel in disguising myself so as to make myself unrecognizable.

ARAMIS
It suffices. You will leave in two hours—that's more than the time necessary to deliver to the Marquise de Montespan what's

she waiting for and to pay a visit to my treasurer.

ASDRUBAL
(joyfully)
Milord's treasurer! Ah! What a pleasure I am going to have to make his acquaintance! This is the first time I've been paid to do a good deed!

(Joel enters.)

ASDRUBAL
(recognizing him, aside)
Mr. Breton.

JOEL
(aside)
My highwayman! What's he doing here?

ARAMIS
(to Asdrubal)
You know this gentleman?

ASDRUBAL
Me, Milord, not very well! By sight alone—from having met him on one of my travels! If it pleases Your Excellency I am going to pass to your treasurer.

ARAMIS
Go! And when you've seen him I advise you not to dally in these parts.

ASDRUBAL
Ah! Milord, I feel very acutely my need to travel.
(He leaves.)

JOEL
(to himself)
What a strange house!
(to Aramis)
Indeed, sir, you spoke of a ceremony—

ARAMIS
It was for that I had you taken in, for that you've reclothed yourself in this outfit that gives you the heroic mind of a Gaiaor or a Don Sanche—which their Majesties will honor with their presence.

JOEL
But still—

ARAMIS
Eh! By Jove, the ceremony of your marriage.

JOEL
(after a moment of stupor, explosively)
But I don't want to get married?

ARAMIS
You don't want to get married?

JOEL
No! A hundred times, a thousand times no!

ARAMIS
Child that you are! Does one resist the will of the king?

JOEL
Is it the King who wants me to get married?

ARAMIS
At least he desires it, and as a respectful subject—

JOEL
Hey! What's the King meddling for? He doesn't know me, he's never seen me.

ARAMIS
Sir, His Majesty knows all the gentlemen of his kingdom—

JOEL
But I'm not a gentleman.

ARAMIS
You will be, if the king wishes it.

JOEL
Still, why this marriage?

ARAMIS
Because every lady in the service of the Queen must be provided with a spouse.

JOEL
So, it's a lady in the service of the Queen that they intend to make me marry like this, with a bag over her head. Well, I am angry for her over it, but if she expects to make me a blockhead, by Jove, by crickey, she's got a good chance of ending without posterity.

ARAMIS
(laughing up his sleeve)
Young man, young monk, take care! The Bastille, you know is a nasty place.

JOEL
Meaning I'll be sent back to it if I refuse to bend to the royal whim! Either marriage or prison! I prefer prison! If my body is confined—my conscience will be at east.

ARAMIS
His Majesty can do more.

JOEL
Yes, I know—he can send me to the scaffold—or the gibbet. He thinks, perhaps, I'm afraid of it. He's mistaken. I was prepared yesterday, I'm prepared today, I'll be prepared tomorrow—does the King want a lesson in courage? Well, let him come to see me die!

ARAMIS
(to himself)
Well said, all that! He's a man—and the cassock of a musketeer would not have been blasphemed on his shoulders! There! There! My young buck! No one wants to do you violence. We are not in Syracuse and Louis the Great has nothing in common with Dionysus, the Tyrant!

JOEL
Pardon me! I'm getting carried away and forgetting what I owe you, what I owe to the kindness of the prince—but I am not clever at disguising my thoughts.

And besides, if you knew—

ARAMIS
If you yourself knew that a fortune is awaiting you—an exquisite creature more charming than the best—

JOEL
I don't desire to know her, for if she was endowed with all human perfections I would rob myself of the happiness of possessing her—you are going to understand me, you, who, being a gentleman, treat a sworn faith as a holy thing—an oath that engages me elsewhere.

ARAMIS
Truly!

JOEL
It's not given twice. I no longer belong to myself.
(noise of clocks)

ARAMIS
Listen—the clocks are pealing for your marriage and what I've told you about brings you a fortune of a dowry, glory, the King's friendship, a post at court and a commission in the army.

JOEL
God is my witness that I've dreamed many times, if not of the honor of commanding soldiers of Mr. de Turenne or Mr. de Condé, at least the joy of marching in their ranks and going to earn before the enemy my brevet as captain or my spurs as chevalier—

ARAMIS
Well?

JOEL
Well, your magician, your enchantress, your fairy, could put me in a situation to realize that dream, still I would refuse!

ARAMIS
Even if this magician, this enchantress, this so-called fairy. Wait, look through this window—that numerous and brilliant entourage—it's the court taking her to the chapel—and there, there—dressed in white—your fiance.

JOEL
(staggering and stuttering after having looked)
Ah! My God! Aurora! It's Aurora!

ARAMIS
Will you refuse her—this one?

JOEL
She! Oh! My God! My God!

ARAMIS
Won't you love her as she deserves to be loved?

JOEL
Yes, I love her! Ah, indeed—look, I am really awake? And she consents to marry me?

ARAMIS
Does it look to you as if she's being dragged to the altar?

JOEL
To marry me! I who have no name!

ARAMIS
Yesterday, perhaps—you were simply Joel—nothing more—today you are the Chevalier Locmaria. Such is the good pleasure of His Majesty.

JOEL
But what have I done to deserve this favor?

ARAMIS
Nothing yet—but I've guaranteed to the King your zeal to serve him. The war isn't over—

JOEL
(with spirit)
Ah! I swear to God that His Majesty will not have a soldier more passionate in defending his flag, or a subject more jealous of his glory. I am ready to pay the debt of gratitude that I am

contracting today—

ARAMIS
I am noting down your words.
(changing tone)
But the only thing missing down there is you. Come on, Chevalier! My God! What a bother to make your happiness.

(They leave.)

CURTAIN

ACT III
SCENE VII

The Departure of Bombardiers.

A crossroads in Saint Germain, rustic pavilion belonging to Paquette, Aramis' hotel to the left. At the rear a gate, completely open to the forest—

BONLARRON
Come, Bistoquet, follow me—

BISTOQUET
I'm here, Boss—

BONLARRON
Call me sergeant.

BISTOQUET
Yes, boss!

PAQUETTE
(as milkmaid)
You here, my godfather—at Saint Germain as a soldier—for goodness sake! Now there's a surprise.

BISTOQUET
And me, too Paquette, here at Saint Germain, but not as a

soldier—huh—that's a surprise too, and agreeable I dare say!

PAQUETTE
Liar, be gone!
(to Bonlarron)
But you—what made you leave your inn?

BONLARRON
Little girl—I've left it definitively.

PAQUETTE
Definitively?

BONLARRON
Yes, I am renouncing giving drink to my contemporaries to take up service in the company of Bombardiers which has just recruited by my former guest, Mr. Petit Renaud.

PAQUETTE
Mr. Petit Renaud! That little red head who was after me like crazy? And you say he just recruited a company?

BONLARRON
Of which he is Captain and who will be, from today, heading toward Freibourg to assist Mr. de Créqui who is in siege operations. That's why we're coming to say our goodbyes to you.

BISTOQUET
Allow me, boss, allow me. Your goodbyes are yours—because as for me, I'm not leaving. As for me, I'm not a warlike man. I like peace, rest, good nourishment. I'm a family man—I adore other people's children.

PAQUETTE
In that case, go get married.

BISTOQUET
Oh, yes, Paquette, still marriage is a lottery. It boasts of many a dupe—

BONLARRON
What, heartlessly, you would allow me to go get killed all alone, when I am consenting to associate you in all my dangers! When I am confiding in you the care of my accoutrements with the title of orderly with the prospect of a corporal's stripes! If enemy bullets have not by then curtailed your progress—

BISTOQUET
But as for me, I don't wish to be curtailed, boss! I don't wish to have familiarity with enemy bullets! Do you see me with an arm or a leg in a sling? No, no, I want to offer Paquette a husband who has all the advantages.

PAQUETTE
It will be vain for you to do so you'll still be lacking something—

BISTOQUET
Of mine! For goodness sake.

PAQUETTE
You will be lacking a mustache, biceps, and character! Are you only susceptible to giving me a slap in the face? Oh! A husband who would be capable of slapping me in the face!

BONLARRON
Here's the Captain.

PETIT RENAUD
(in uniform)
At last, I have company! God's blood, magnificent men! The Colossus of Rhodes is not going to be as huge as I.

PAQUETTE
You are superb in war uniform.

PETIT RENAUD
I am handsome, aren't I? Yes, the beauties are directing their eyes against me. The ladies of Saint Germain know good looking men. What I regret is the absence of friend, Joel.

PAQUETTE
That little blonde pleased me greatly. I would willingly have had a soft spot for him.

BISTOQUET
Oh! You, you have a soft spot for everybody except for me.

PETIT RENAUD
We are marching in an hour. The route is long—it's more than 100 leagues from here to Freibourg.

BONLARRON
A stroll to awaken the appetite. In the Ferte Regiment—in the Flanders campaign we saw many such.

PAQUETTE
Captain, are you passing back this way when you leave?

PETIT RENAUD
Many times, my beauty—the first detachment will leave from here.

PAQUETTE
Well, in that case, in my turn I am preparing a surprise for you.

THE THREE OTHERS
A surprise!

PAQUETTE
Yes, a surprise. I'll only tell you this—and I am leaving you. But you will see me again, yes, damn it, you will see me again. Sonofabitch! Jesus Christ!
(she goes in)

BISTOQUET
Oh! How she swears.

PETIT RENAUD
You, Sergeant Bonlarron, in the absence of the Lieutenant, go fetch our men at the Commissary and bring them together in this square.

BONLARRON
I am going there, my Captain. Follow me, volunteer Bistoquet.

BISTOQUET
Volunteer—by force—wow!

(They leave by the back.)

PETIT RENAUD
(reading some papers)
Yes, all is in order. I won't wait any longer for my second, a young ensign recommended to me by Mr. Colbert, who himself charged me with giving him his commission.
(he removes the brevet, and places the other papers in his pocket)
Let's see.
(reading the signature)
"The Chevalier de Locmaria, at the hotel of the Spanish Ambassador at Saint Germain! The hotel—there it is here! But the Chevalier de Locmaria—who is this man?
(rings the hotel bell)
That name tells me nothing. Possibly, because I've never heard it.

(to Bazin who appears)
Is this indeed where the Chevalier de Locmaria resides?

BAZIN
It's here!

PETIT RENAUD
Eh! That's not you, for sure? Fine! Lead me to him right away.

BAZIN
Impossible, Captain. The Chevalier is not at the hotel.

PETIT RENAUD
Not at the hotel? And where is he?

BAZIN
The Chevalier is getting married.

PETIT RENAUD
Not possible! Today?
(noise of clocks)

BAZIN
At his very moment.

PETIT RENAUD
And he's not at the hotel but at the altar?

BAZIN
The Chevalier won't be long.

PETIT RENAUD
I'm going to wait for him here. Is he going to be nonplussed to learn he's spending his night with me and not his bride? Poor Chevalier! Now he interests me. If he marries a plain Jane he will perhaps be enchanted.

(drums off)
Ah! Ah! Here come my men.

THE POPULACE
There they are! There they are!

(Bonlarron has entered at the head of his company and marched up in order before Petit Renaud.)

BONLARRON
Halt! Front!
(the company is at the right, oblique to the audience)

FIRST GOSSIP
(to his neighbor)
See, sweetie, the cannoneers.

BISTOQUET
(as a soldier)
No, my brave woman, Bombardiers! The first detachment of Bombardiers of Captain Petit Renaud inventor of bombs!

SECOND GOSSIP
And where are you going to?

BISTOQUET
We are going to take Freibourg my little chickadee!

THIRD GOSSIP
That's fine for you, for handsome men, it's all handsome men.

BISTOQUET
What's she mean fine for me! Oh! She doesn't know anything about it.

BONLARRON
(calling)
Bistoquet!

BISTOQUET
Boss!

BONLARRON
Call me Sergeant. My niece has promised us a surprise. Where is she?

BISTOQUET
I'm waiting for her boss.

PETIT RENAUD
Do better. Go get her.

PAQUETTE
(opening the door and appearing dressed as a canteen girl)
Here's the surprise!

PETIT RENAUD and BONLARRON
Paquette as a vivandière!

PAQUETTE
Yes, comrades, I'm taking up the uniform and maternal casks to keep you company.

ALL
Bravo.

PAQUETTE
If the Captain permits.

PETIT RENAUD
Yes, I permit it.

BISTOQUET
Paquette leaving! That decides my vocation—cause—
(singing)
Out of sight, out of mind.
That's what the proverb says.

BONLARRON
But, Paquette, you are lacking a donkey! All vivandières have a donkey.

PAQUETTE
(pointing to Bistoquet)
Well, there he is. I'm attaching Bistoquet to myself in that capacity.
(all laugh)

BISTOQUET
Me! A disciple of Apollo—

PAQUETTE
Yes! Meanwhile, Bombardier Bistoquet, help me to pay welcome to all these brave folks.
(she distributes goblets assisted by Bistoquet and some soldiers)

ALL
Long live the Vivandière of the Bombardiers!

PAQUETTE
(pouring)
Regale yourselves, my friends.

PETIT RENAUD
Yes, gang, regale yourselves! That's not a reason, praise God! Because the Bombardiers are at pains not to take the parting cup.

(The soldiers are grouped around the characters)

PETIT RENAUD
(singing)
Wine awakens courage.
Let's drink the parting cup!
At the bottom of the glass is hope
Let's drink to the best Bombardier in France!

BISTOQUET
It's proud to be a soldier—

BONLARRON
Especially a bombardier!

BISTOQUET
Wherever you go, in love, in war—

BONLARRON
The Bombardiers are number one!

PETIT RENAUD
So go forward, head held high—
All give way to their conquering assault.
Praise god! Everything's in flame, everything's hopping—
Hearts as well as citadels.
Wine awakes (etc.)

BISTOQUET
Under the fine uniform I wear—

BONLARRON
Under this brocade—

BISTOQUET
I feel a hero's soul within.

BONLARRON
I've got the heart of a Field Marshal.

PAQUETTE
For you I bring wine
In my late mama's casks.
Always place me
At the head of the regiment!
Wine awakens, etc.

(The bells are ringing. Joel and Aurora appear at the back. They exchange greetings with the Lords and the Ladies and then come forward. Aramis and Boislaurier remain at the back.)

BAZIN
(to Petit Renaud)
Captain, here is the Chevalier de Locmaria.

(He points Joel out to him.)

PETIT RENAUD
My lieutenant! Great! I am going to greet him as he passes.

(Joel is looking at Aurora in a way that Petit Renaud cannot see him from where he has posted himself before the door of Aramis' hotel.)

JOEL
(to Aurora)
Aurora, my darling Aurora here we are at last together.

AURORA
Yes, I have difficulty in believing that happiness has so suddenly arrived. This tornado of events is giving me vertigo!

JOEL
Just like me when I learned you had agreed to be my wife. The excess of my happiness almost made me go crazy. But since it is real, let's savor it without unease and without fear, God who has just received our oaths permits us.

(They have arrived at the gate of the hotel which lackeys have opened wide.)

PETIT RENAUD
She's no plain Jane.
(aloud)
Pardon! The Chevalier de Locmaria?

JOEL
(raising his head)
That's me, sir.

PETIT RENAUD
Joel!

JOEL
Petit Renaud.
(they hug each other)
Aurora, it's Petit Renaud. My friend Petit Renaud who valiantly aided me the other day in driving off the bandits—you recollect him?

PETIT RENAUD
(bowing to Aurora)
Madame, receive my homage and my compliments.
(to Joel)
Married! Happy—and there I was thinking you were caged up! Yes, in evidence of which, I proposed, once Freibourg was consumed in flames by my invention to demand your pardon from the King as a reward—and if he had refused me, to make

the Bastille jump to get you out of there, still with my invention.

JOEL
Renaud, my brave Renaud, how happy I am over this unexpected meeting! But why are you speaking of burning Freibourg? Explain yourself, I don't understand.

PETIT RENAUD
What do you mean you don't understand? Wearing the uniform you are wearing—such as mine—

ARAMIS
(coming forward)
A delicate attention of the King who before you even received your commission, because in the sight of this uniform sent your nomination in the grade of lieutenant, in your friend's new company.

PETIT RENAUD
The bombardiers of Captain, Petit Renaud. Yes, Joel, Mr. Colbert has had executed from my plans, mortars and bombs which he is sending us to experiment with in Freibourg and I am charged with delivering you your commission. Here it is.
(giving him the Brevet)

JOEL
(reading it rapidly)
Officer! I'm an officer!

BISTOQUET
All our congratulations, Chevalier.

DE MAUPERTIUS
(enters exhibiting a second order sealed with the royal seal)
Order from His Majesty!

JOEL
(after having read it)
Why, it's not possible! No, Lord God, this is not possible—what His Majesty is asking of me!

DE MAUPERTIUS
His Majesty doesn't ask—His Majesty commands, sir.

AURORA
What is it?

JOEL
Listen, my dear soul, listen, my friends.
(he reads)
"As soon as these presents are received, the Chevalier de Locmaria will leave for Paris where he will report immediately to Mr. Louvois our minster of war—The latter shall deliver to him dispatches which he will take in all diligence to Marshal de Créqui before Freibourg. No delay, under whatever pretext can be adduced to the accomplishment of this mission. Mr. de Maupertius, the Captain of our guards is charged with putting the aforesaid Chevalier de Locmaria on route.
Signed Louis."

DE MAUPERTIUS
Well?

JOEL
Well—His Majesty wasn't thinking. He must have forgotten—no question. What the devil! I cannot leave like this in the evening my wife that he gave me in the morning.

DE MAUPERTIUS
You are a soldier, sir, and obedience.

JOEL
Take me to the King. I want to speak to him, to tell him—

DE MAUPERTIUS
Impossible. By now you ought to be already en route to Paris.

PETIT RENAUD
(coming up to Joel)
Alas! Mr. Maupertius is right. And you behold me distressed because I am the cause of what is happening to you.

JOEL
You?

PETIT RENAUD
Hey! Yes—not suspecting that it would so soon be put to the test I had unlucky idea of telling the King about the ardent zeal with which you are burning for his service. Did I depict with too much eloquence how impatient you were to give proof of it! Was I wrong, at last, to repeat to him your words of pledge?

AURORA
Ah! Mr. de Locmaria has taken a pledge?

PETIT RENAUD
Pledging to sacrifice all his interests to his country and his promise.

JOEL
That's true—but I didn't know—in the name of heaven, advise me.

PETIT RENAUD
(gravely)
Child, it is in such circumstances that a man of courage must look to his own counsel.

DE MAUPERTIUS
In short, what shall I tell the King?

JOEL
What do you say, Aurora?

AURORA
Did you think that I love you so ill and that I would have so little care of your glory that I would seek to retain you? Honor demands it. Leave!

JOEL
What—it's you who—

AURORA
Leave! You offered your services to France! It is not possible for you to refuse them when France calls for them. Go, then, Joel—no hesitation, no weakness! This thought that each of us is doing his duty, will console both of us—you in the course of a "long voyage" and I here in my solitude.

PETIT RENAUD
Blast it! Courageous little woman!

BOISLAURIER
(low to Aramis)
She's comes to our assistance marvelously.

PETIT RENAUD
(low)
By Jove! Wherever there's a woman there lies man's ruin!

JOEL
(to Aramis)
Thanks, Duke!
(to Aurora)

Thanks, O you guardian of my honor! You have dictated my conduct.
(to Petit Renaud)
Captain, I am at your orders.

(Petit Renaud makes a sign to Bonlarron, who puts the company underarms.)

BONLARRON
Arms!
(roll of drums)

AURORA
You are taking my whole soul with you.

JOEL
I love you!
(to Aramis)
Take her, sir—take her—and receive my goodbyes. It's to you that I confide her.

(Aramis goes into the hotel and soon appears with Aurora on the balcony of the hotel. Meanwhile Bistoquet has shut the shutters on the window of the shop and posted a notice.)

BISTOQUET
(pointing to the sign)
Look and read! "Closed because of patriotism!"

PETIT RENAUD
Now, going on to Freibourg! By the left, left! Right turn—forward, March.
(The Column marches off, resuming the refrain of the song, the populace has run in shouting, "Long live the bombardiers! Aurora sends a kiss to Joel from her balcony.)

Freeze as the curtain falls.

CURTAIN

ACT IV
SCENE VIII

Créqui's camp.

The stage represents the end tip of a camp supported by trenches in the way of being dug out to the left, obliquely and lost in the trees, some tents, between the tents, horses that the Chevaliers in lieu of a stable are busy grooming. To the right, at the back also seen obliquely a trench through which bombardiers and light cavalry are traveling pell mell—a mortar has been set up—others are waiting at back.

At rise: The action takes place at the rear, most of the stage being empty. Officers are there. The workers near the ramp are all cavaliers. To the left, Paquette's canteen.

CHEVALIERS
(together)
That's enough!
Try harder! The devil.

DE LA BERANGE
(a captain)
Well, what's wrong?

FIRST CAVALIER
Captain—the Marshal is making fun of us—

DE LA BERANGE
Bah!

FIRST CAVALIER
Yes, not satisfied with transforming us into foot soldiers and to make us servants of the artillery, behold, today he's changing us into ditch diggers.

SECOND CAVALIER
They take our swords and muskets from us to replace them with pick axes and spades.

FIRST CAVALIER
By God! It wasn't for nothing that the King put spurs on our boots and horses under us! Just let them give us the order to charge squares of pike men or on cannons that cough up death, in the saddle, bridle in hand, and foot in the stirrup—we will go to it, like we went to it at Hochborg, serving the imperial horsemen! But to shovel sand, excavate tunnels, do a mole's work—

SECOND CAVALIER
Never! Never! These tools! Let's break them.

PETIT RENAUD
(covered with dirt emerges from the trench—to Mr. de Berange)
God's belly! Sir, I think your men are mutinying.

DE LA BERANGE
As you see, sir! They are refusing absolutely to do what you exact of them. Anyway this work gang is so outside of the ordinary usages that I am making bold to a dispensation from Marshal Créqui for my cavaliers. Meanwhile seek the workers you need elsewhere.

(Approval by the Cavaliers.)

PETIT RENAUD
And I, sir, I repeat to you, that I've received an order from Major General de Basset, in command of the artillery, to take command of your men, to help me complete this trench and to install my battery. And God be praised, I will take them, even if I must grab each one of them by their collar to lead them to the work.

(Disgruntled murmurs from the Cavaliers.)

PETIT RENAUD
Come on! You with the unkempt uniform—get this pick in hand and set an example.

(The Cavalier doesn't budge.)

PETIT RENAUD
Eh! You didn't hear me?

FIRST CAVALIER
Deed I did.

PETIT RENAUD
Then obey!

FIRST CAVALIER
I only obey officers.

PETIT RENAUD
Praise God! Am I not an officer?

FIRST CAVALIER
Our officers!

(Laughter from the Cavaliers.)

PETIT RENAUD
(calling)
Sergeant Bonlarron.

BONLARRON
(emerging form the tent)
Arrest this big gawky fellow and take him for me with four guards to the Provost who will deal with him.

BONLARRON
Fine, Captain, hey! Four mean at arms.

(Threatening murmurs from the Cavaliers.)

DE LA BERANGE
(to Petit Renaud)
Sir! Sir! Trust me don't persist for I warn you my light cavalry will not allow the arrest of their comrade.

CAVALIERS
No! No!

PETIT RENAUD
That's what we shall see! Help me, My Bombardiers!

(The Bombardiers leave through the trench with their spades and their axes and arrange themselves, ready to support their Captain.)

DE LA BERANGE
One more time, sir, I am holding you responsible for the blood that's going to be spilled.

PETIT RENAUD
And as for me, I am holding you responsible for the rebellion and insolence of your Cavaliers—mutineers that I will have

punished commencing with their Captain.

(He draws his sword, De la Berange imitates him, they cross swords. The Bombardiers and the light horse begin to pitch into each other.)

(Joel all covered with dust a pick axe in his hand emerges from the trench and rushes excitedly between the Cavaliers and the Bombardiers.)

JOEL
One moment! One moment! Get back, everybody! And you gentlemen, put up! You don't need your swords to listen to me.

PETIT RENAUD
You want—?

DE LA BERANGE
You intend—?

JOEL
I wish and I intend to tell you that you are both all wrong!

PETIT RENAUD
Wrong?

DE LA BERANGE
The two of us?

JOEL
(calmly to Petit Renaud)
You, first of all, my comrade, you have such imperious manners and so aggressive to demand a thing, that were one as sweet as a sheep, one would always want to send you to the devil! As for you, my Captain, allow me to declare to you with all deference and with all frankness, that you've committed a serious fault,

you and your men, by refusing to execute the orders of a major general.

DE LA BERANGE
Sir!

JOEL
(to Cavaliers)
Aren't you servants of the King when you have a horse under you? Are you centaurs or soldiers? And do you think, to be on foot one works less effectively for the flag of France? Eh! What were you sent to do here, gentlemen? Light Cavalrymen, you, like these brave folks, like me, like the whole army? To help the Marshal take Freibourg! Well, let's all help him. Help him above all by sacrificing to him idle vanity and a stupid esprit de corps! Go, to storm the fortress, a blow with the pick axe is as valuable as a blow with a saber! And there's no less honor in pushing a wheelbarrow under enemy fire, than maneuvering a squadron while razing the countryside against a battery or a battalion.

(A bullet lands on embankment just behind Joel. A sack stops it and covers Joel with dust.)

JOEL
Do you understand now the usefulness of the work you are directed to perform? Without these sandbags that bullet would have fallen in our midst!

(Two balls land a bit further away. Mr. de la Berange utters a scream and falls.)

JOEL
(rushing to him)
Dead.
(to soldiers)

Bad luck! If the front of the trench had been covered to the end, this brave gentleman would still be alive!

VOICE OF CAVALIERS
It's true! It's true!

JOEL
Two of you carry this officer to the ambulance, and all the rest follow me.

ALL
Yes! Yes! Into the trench! Everybody!

BISTOQUET
(emerging from the canteen)
Yes, yes, into the trench! Into the trench! Yes, everybody.

PAQUETTE
Not you, Bistoquet, you shan't go!

BISTOQUET
(removing his vest)
I shall go! I heard Mr. Joel. He put the devil into me. To take the fortress a blow with the pick axe is as valuable as a saber blow—! I am a pick man, I am!

PAQUETTE
You shan't go, I tell you! You've been ordered to help me with the labors of the canteen and I intend that you help me. To take the fortress the officers of the company need nourishment, and to nourish them, a bit of sweat is worth a blow with the pick.

BISTOQUET
Well, Miss Paquette, sweat by yourself. As for me, I'm going to dig.
(he heads toward the trench)

PAQUETTE
Can you understand him! To go get himself killed when nothing forces you to do it! Why he's changed on me, my Bistoquet!
(running in front of him and barring his way)
And as for me, I say you will not pass—

BISTOQUET
Get out of the way, or if not—
(threatening)

PAQUETTE
Ah! He's great like this! How coaxing he is!

BISTOQUET
Come on! Quicker than that to the canteen—come on, come on, and don't argue. You are beginning to warm my ears.

PAQUETTE
Uncle, godfather—help!

BISTOQUET
(raising his hand)
Will you shut up or do I slap you?

BONLARRON
(at the entrance to the trench)
Well! What's wrong here?

PAQUETTE
(weeping)
Boo! Hoo! He raised his hand.
(changing tone)
It's nothing, godfather.

BISTOQUET
Nothing at all!

PAQUETTE
I'm very content.

BISTOQUET
And me, too.
(sings)
When love occupies us—
One is either deserver or deserved.

BONLARRON
In that case, why are you arguing, if the two of you are very content?

PAQUETTE
We are not disputing! It was happiness, joy, emotion.

BISTOQUET
(aside)
She's got some nerve, for goodness sake!

PAQUETTE
And I was calling you to tell you I've just decided.

BONLARRON
To do what?

PAQUETTE
To give my hand to Bistoquet.

BISTOQUET
(aside)
Oh! My God!

PAQUETTE
To Bistoquet who just carried off my head like a grenade pouch.
(blowing him kisses)

Here, love! Here, darling! And to ask for your consent and blessing.

BISTOQUET
(going to Paquette)
Ah, Paquette.
(sings)
Oh, yes, my joy is great.
I hold my beauty from herself.

BONLARRON
Well, niece, you pick a funny time!

PAQUETTE
Godfather, one doesn't choose! It happens when it happens!

BISTOQUET
(aside)
All the same, she told him that she would only love a husband capable of—

BONLARRON
(placing them hand in hand)
Come, approach, scamp! Under enemy fire I crown you here.

BISTOQUET
A poem! You are also a poet in that case?

BONLARRON
Me? Well, without knowing it! Children, I give you my blessing.

SENTINEL
To arms! The Marshal.

(De Créqui enters on foot with officers and soldiers.)

JOEL and PETIT RENAUD
(emerging from the trench)
The Marshal.
(they try to clean up.}

MARSHAL
Don't try to fix your clothes, gentlemen! This appearance does you honor. Night is approaching and Freibourg has ceased its fire. Let your workers rest until tomorrow morning.

I congratulate the company of Bombardiers. It's with a succession of such labors that little by little we are approaching the fortress, whose capture will end this harsh campaign. Yes, gentlemen! The ending is up there between those towers, from which Prince Charles contemplates rushing to ravish Lorraine from us. But this impenetrable town, we will take it, if I have to throw my Marshal's baton into these formidable defenses.

JOEL
(with enthusiasm)
We will all go to find it, Marshal.

PETIT RENAUD
Yes, all—Praise God!

OFFICERS and SOLDIERS
All! All! To Freibourg! To Freibourg!

JOEL
Let's go there right away then.

OFFICERS and SOLDIERS
That's it right away! The assault! The assault!

MARSHAL
Young folks—bravery but no rashness! Can you see from here

that citadel fastened like an eagle's nest on the side of the mountain?

That's what they call the château. That's what you are talking of taking as if you had wings to mount to it, or as if I had a hypogriff to carry you there! No, by Jove, be patient. Let us play with mines, tunnels, and cannon! Once a breech is opened it won't be your general keeping you back!

On the contrary, it's he who will be showing you the way.

JOEL
Yes—but when will that breach be opened?

MARSHAL
Lieutenant, you are more curious than I am knowledgeable and that question—

JOEL
(crudely)
Ah! Because you see, Marshal—if things drag on like this much longer—

MARSHAL
Well—?

JOEL
Well, I will be obliged to take the place myself.
(general hilarity)

MARSHAL
Yeah! And I who thought that in this company of Musketeers only the Captain was a Gaston.
(pinching Joel)
So be it, Lieutenant, don't get upset! If you have an idea for doing it better and faster than we do, you'll be supplied with the

means of putting it into action.

JOEL
I don't have that idea yet, Marshal. But don't worry—it will come to me.

MARSHAL
(good naturedly)
In that case, hurry to have it.

PETIT RENAUD
(to Joel)
I will help you, comrade.

JOEL
(to Petit Renaud)
Ah, yes, an idea! Find an idea! And then I'll return to France, to Saint Germain—where al my desires, my regrets and my hopes fly to.

OFFICER
(entering)
Marshal Créqui.

MARSHAL
What is it, sir—

OFFICERS
The scouts just arrested an old geezer who wandered into sight of our lines. He protests his innocence and insists on having the honor of seeing you—stating he has a request to address you.

MARSHAL
Have him brought here.
(the officer leaves)
Some spy—no question!

(two soldiers lead in an old man who can barely walk, leaning on a cane)

OFFICER
There he is, Marshal—

MARSHAL
You have a request to present me?

ASDRUBAL
Mr. Marshal you can do me the greatest service.

MARSHAL
Explain yourself—

ASDRUBAL
I am a peaceful bourgeois of the city you are besieging.

MARSHAL
Of Freibourg?

ASDRUBAL
Yes, Mr. Marshal. A month ago I left my hearth to go to Paris where I wanted to consult a knowledgeable doctor on the subject of my daughter, a girl of 16, Mr. Marshal. I have only her and she's dying—of the same illness that ravished her mother! Alas, science is powerless—and perhaps it's a shroud I am going to find in the doorway of my house.

BONLARRON
A thousand pikes! The poor fellow moves me.

ASDRUBAL
Oh! How long the road seemed to me, to return towards my beloved dying girl! Finally, I arrive, here before me, the walls behind which are my last affections and I cannot approach

them! The war stands between her and me! Inexorable war! War which is going to steal from me perhaps the last sigh of my daughter—

MARSHAL
If I've understood you correctly, your wish would be to enter Freibourg!

ASDRUBAL
(bursting into tears)
In the name of heaven, have pity! Think of that unfortunate creature who's going to leave me forever is there, a few paces from her father and that each minute that goes by robs me of a chance to see her again. Pity, Marshal, pity!

PETIT RENAUD
God's blood! Praise God! God's belly! I am weeping like a child of a young heifer.

JOEL
And as for me, I don't know why that man says nothing good to me!
(aside)
Where the devil have I heard that voice?

MARSHAL
Prudence, sir, does not exclude humanity.
(calling)
Mr. Locmaria!
(movement by the old geezer)
You are going to place yourself in communication with the enemy, by hoisting the flag and trumpeting for a parley.

JOEL
Fine, my Marshal.

ASDRUBAL and JOEL
(recognizing each other, aside)
Him!

MARSHAL
(to Asdrubal)
The Lieutenant will accompany you.
(to Joel)
You will deliver this man to those of the besieged who meet with you—and you will return to our lines leaving him in their hands.
(to Asdrubal)
Wasn't this what you wanted from me?

ASDRUBAL
Oh, thanks, Mr. Marshal, thanks.
(to Joel)
Come, sir, come quickly.

MARSHAL
One moment—before giving you satisfaction a formality has to be accomplished that the laws of war impose on us. Mr. de Locmaria will escort you to the Provost where you will be searched, after that you'll be blindfolded so as to cross our attack front—

ASDRUBAL
Let them search me, Mr. Marshal! I don't fear a thing.

JOEL
(approaching Asdrubal)
My brave man, I ask your pardon if I am going to delay for a few minutes your family effusions. But it seems to me that, for an old geezer, you lean very lightly on a cane.

(He kicks Asdrubal's cane away—Asdrubal makes a violent

gesture to get it back.)

ASDRUBAL
My cane!
(aside)
The devil!

JOEL
(imitating Asdrubal's voice)
"You see, Milord, no more letter—vanished."

ASDRUBAL
(terrified)
He knows everything.

JOEL
(continuing and picking up the cane)
"And then who would suspect the cane of a poor old geezer."
(unscrewing the pommel of the cane and pulling out the letter)
My Marshal—here's a message that this honest father of a family was bearing to the governor of Freibourg.

ASDRUBAL
Ah! Demon!
(he makes a desperate effort to seize the paper)

JOEL
(flooring him)
One moment, Master Asdrubal de Cordeboeuff—! One Minute! And show us your villainous fare!
(pulling of his beard and wig—

ASDRUBAL
Lost!

JOEL
Marshal, shall I strangle the reptile?

MARSHAL
Control yourself, Lieutenant! He belongs to my provost—
(perusing the letter)
Yes, this is really it—a note promising them help before long—and announcing to them that Prince Charles is marching to enclose us in a circle of steel.
So well—
(pointing to Joel)
That without for this brave lad, it's not we who will take Freibourg but Freibourg that would take us—! By the devil! Do you think, gentlemen, I am justified in the judgment, I am going to give? Hola! Mr. Provost.
(the Provost presents himself. Pointing out Asdrubal)
Hang this man for me, immediately!
(the Provost makes a sign four solders and Bonlarron seizes Asdrubal)

BONLARRON
(pushing him)
Let's go! March!

ASDRUBAL
Hanged! Like papa! No luck in this family.
(they leave)

MARSHAL
So much for the messenger! As for the message.
(he makes a face as if to tear it up)

JOEL
(grabbing his arm)
Oh! Marshal, give it to me!

MARSHAL
And what do you want to do with it?

JOEL
(lowering his voice)
It's the key that will open the gates of Freibourg to us.

MARSHAL
(after a moment of reflection)
Than take it, Lieutenant, but be prudent!

JOEL
Hey, Marshal, there's something we have that's greater than prudence: Courage! Tomorrow, as dawn is born, see it, your eagle's nest! If the standard of France is not floating up there from the top of this tower crowning the castle, it's I who will be dead! But don't worry, I will live! I want to see my wife too much!

ALL
Long live Joel! Long live Joel!

CURTAIN

ACT IV
SCENE IX

The French Transgression.

A small room in the tower of the fortress. Side doors. Open window on the left.

GENERAL SCHUTZ
This inaction by the enemy does not fail to make me uneasy. Marshal de Créqui is a tricky customer. No question he's preparing a surprise for us. Luckily, we lack neither munitions nor supplies—our garrison is solid and the population appears to be animated with the best morale. And then, Duke Charles has promised to come to raise the siege. He will do as he said!

FIRST OFFICER
(coming in)
General, a messenger who pretends to come from Paris.

GENERAL SCHUTZ
A messenger? From Paris? And how did he get here? I imagine that the besiegers didn't let him pass peacefully through their lines. And at least he didn't fall from the firmament—astride the moon.

FIRST OFFICER
Pursued by French musket fire, he hurled himself in the moat

shouting to us—friend—so I took it upon myself to toss a cord to him and hoist him up to the bastion!

GENERAL SCHUTZ
Very fine. Have him brought to me.

(Joel and his escort enter. Joel is in the dress, wig and beard of Asdrubal. He imitates the senile behavior of Asdrubal.)

GENERAL SCHUTZ
(abruptly)
Where are you coming from?

JOEL
From Paris!

GENERAL SCHUTZ
You say you are bearer of a message to the governor of Freibourg?
(nod by Joel)
I am General Schutz—governor of Freibourg—deliver your message to me.

JOEL
(presenting the note from Aramis)
Here it is!

GENERAL SCHUTZ
(opening it)
From the Spanish Ambassador.
(he peruses it)

JOEL
(aside)
Here I am in the heart of the place—careful! But bah! It would really be the devil if a Breton from Belle Isle didn't succeed in duping this fat fellow.

GENERAL SCHUTZ
(to the officers)
Well, what did I tell you, gentlemen? That our ally wouldn't leave us in the lurch? Here's the Spanish Ambassador advising me from Paris that the Duke of Lorrain is on the march to take the French from the rear.

JOEL
(rubbing his hands)
That's it! A double attack—simultaneously—on one side Prince Charles and his troops—on the other the garrison and population of Freibourg along with their governor! Marshal Créqui won't be able to resist!

GENERAL SCHUTZ
The French are lost.
(he talks with his officers)

JOEL
(aside)
At least the bombs of Petit Renaud aren't coming to reverse the roles!

GENERAL SCHUTZ
(to his officers)
I won't detain you, gentlemen. It's night! You may withdraw.

(The officers leave.)

GENERAL SCHUTZ
(patting Joel on the shoulder)
What's your name, friend?

JOEL
The glorious Asdrubal is my patron!

GENERAL SCHUTZ
Well, Squire Asdrubal, I am inviting you to supper and we will click glasses together in celebration of this fine news.

JOEL
General, that will be a great honor for a poor old geezer like me!
(aside)
Petit Renaud don't budge yet.

GENERAL SCHUTZ
(at back)
Two place settings.

(Two soldiers bring in a small table.)

JOEL
(aside)
Still it was quite agreed that an hour after my entry into Freibourg he would make a diversion trying this bombs at the other end of the city.

GENERAL SCHUTZ
(to Asdrubal)
To table, Squire Asdrubal.
(he installs himself in the armchair)
Come, sit here, facing me, and to your health—my venerable old friend.

JOEL
To yours, my general!

GENERAL SCHUTZ
So you are in the service—

JOEL
In the service of Spanish Ambassador.

(aside)
Ah! Petit Renaud! Petit Renaud!

GENERAL SCHUTZ
But how did you succeed in crossing the French lines?

JOEL
Oh! The French do not have a lot of suspicion.

GENERAL SCHUTZ
(laughing)
I know. I know. They drink with the devil without noticing his horns.

JOEL
As you say.
(clinking)
Here's to you, General.

GENERAL SCHUTZ
And to you!

JOEL
(coughing)
I beg your pardon. That forced bath I had to take in the moat—
(aside)
What can Petit Renaud be doing?
(he looks out the window)

GENERAL SCHUTZ
A nice dive, huh?
(pause)
This tower is the culminating point of the fortress, and the observatory from which I follow all the activity of the French! Ah! You can boast of having a fine escape!
(great uproar of a cannonade)

JOEL
(aside)
Ah! At last.

GENERAL SCHUTZ
(rising)
Well, now what is that?

JOEL
An attack.

FIRST OFFICER
(entering)
My general, the French weary of bombarding the chateau and are now hurling their balls on the town. The inhabitants are going mad.

SECOND OFFICER
(entering)
The troops themselves are losing control. For these projectile are of a new type which explode when they touch the soil.

JOEL
(with joy)
Brave—brave—Petit Renaud.

GENERAL SCHUTZ
(officers)
I am with you.
(to Joel, while putting on his sword)
Squire Asdrubal, no one will disturb you. They are guarding outside carefully.
(sneering)
There's no other exit but this window.

JOEL
Till we meet again, General!

GENERAL SCHUTZ
(to his officers)
Let's go, gentlemen—

(Schutz carefully locks the door. Joel runs to be sure of it.)

JOEL
Locked!
(looking through the keyhole)
Outside, soldier in arms—above the guard corps! The general didn't lie. I am well-guarded. Come on, by the Grace of God! To the devil with these old clothes.
(he quickly removes his wig and Asdrubal's clothing)
Oof! Come what may! I prefer myself this way! To say that at this moment, Bonlarron and his valiant squad are taking a foot bath in the moat!
(takes a lamp and waves it in the window)
Quick! The signal they are waiting for. Once they've seen it, a trumpet will sound over the fire.
(he listens)
Nothing! Let's wait!
(he places the lamp on the window sill then pulls form his breast a package of rope which he begins to unroll.
The ladders are below. It's a question of hauling them up here. Let's see, I need something heavy enough at the end of this rope to hurl it more surely. Ah, this bottle.
(he takes the bottle and ties it to the end of the rope. In the distance, covering fire is heard)
Finally they've seen the signal!
(he runs to the window and raises the lamp)
Brave friends.
(returning)
Where are they?

Ah! I see their motionless silhouettes. To work!
(he hurls the empty bottle and the cord attached to it. A distant noise of cord breaking against the rocks is heard and Joel attaches the cord to the crossbar of the window)
Aurora, my dear wife, in the beautiful country of France where you are waiting for me, pray God to be merciful to these brave men who are devoted to their country and ask him to bring you back your Joel!
(he returns to the window and tries to pull the rope)
Ah! The rope resists! They've attached the ladders! Let's pull them!
(pulling the rope as if fetching water from a well. Noise outside)
A few more minutes! Give me time, Lord God.

(The door opens abruptly. Schutz enters and speaks to his officers who remain outside)

GENERAL SCHUTZ
Nothing's to be done against an enemy protected by night! Let the inhabitants remain closed in their houses, and let the troops rest until dawn! They'll need to be solid to sustain Marshal Créqui's assault, if he delivers it, or to attack him if he does not! Till later, gentlemen! In two hours I will take command.
(he locks the door with a double lock)

(Joel has not ceased to hoist his rope. He pulls up two ladders which he attaches firmly to the crossbar of the window.)

GENERAL SCHUTZ
Squire Asdrubal! Hey, who are you?
(he moves toward the door. Joel puts himself quickly before the door, whose key he takes and trains a pistol on Schutz)

JOEL
Who am I? A Frenchman who sat at your table, General, and who for that reason would rather not kill you!

GENERAL SCHUTZ
(threatening)
A Frenchman! What were you doing at this window?

JOEL
(playfully)
My God! I was line fishing in the depths of the moat.

GENERAL SCHUTZ
And what were you fishing for?

JOEL
Oh! For Frenchies! Little Frenchies! They're biting, General, they're biting.

GENERAL SCHUTZ
(rushing toward the window)
Wretch!

GENERAL SCHUTZ
(deflecting him)
By crickey! Don't touch those ropes! It's dangerous.

GENERAL SCHUTZ
Help me! Help me!

JOEL
(keeping his pistol in his hand)
Eh! Call! Call! Before they've had time to come to your aid, I'll have had the time to dispatch you ten times.

GENERAL SCHUTZ
(pulling his sword)
We're going to see about that.

JOEL
(skittering behind the table)
Instead, listen to me, General. You are coming unbeknownst to you to play a bet with me for which Freibourg is the prize. You've lost. Pay up like a good gambler! And I promise you, my word as an officer and a gentleman to obtain for you and yours honorable conditions from Marshal Créqui.

GENERAL SCHUTZ
(attacking him)
Never, French puppy! Never!

JOEL
Never!
(he aims his pistol, then thinking twice putting down his weapon)
No a shot would give the alarm.
(putting out the lamp)
To luck—!

GENERAL SCHUTZ
Well—you're the one who asked for it!

(Joel turns over the lamp. Complete darkness. Schultz, sword in hand, seeks his adversary. This one takes the greatcoat of Asdrubal off which he had divested himself, and uses it like a shield, and ends by throwing it over the head of Schutz who he grabs by the arm and floors. Desperate struggle.)

JOEL
Useless for you to fight, general. This fist is that of Porthos—
(he drags him to the window)
Look out below!
(he hurls him out)
My excuses General; I indeed told you that it was dangerous!

CURTAIN

ACT IV
SCENE X

The scaling.

Complete night, starlight, by which can be seen, vaguely at first, then plainly a large tower.

It's the exterior of the tower in which the action of the preceding scene took place. Two rope ladders can be seen which are lost in the heights.

A means of descent is open. From this depth the voices of Bonlarron and his companions are heard. The tower is lost in the vault where Joel's voice is also heard.

BONLARRON
(from above)
The ladders are in position, are you ready?

VOICE
We are ready.

BONLARRON
Then listen up! Musket on your back.
(one soon notices a soldier's head, then body, and the tower begins to descend)
Do like me at each rung, breathe—

Look up—not down!
Don't think of danger, but of France.

JOEL
(from above)
Of France.

BONLARRON
Of France! That's Joel's voice! Be good, my friends! Hoist, Bistoquet.

BISTOQUET
Here, Boss!
(sings)
In love, like glory, you have to be sincere.

(The tower continues to be lowered until the window from whose crossbars the ladders are attached appears. Joel is leaning from the window and extending his hands to the soldiers.)

JOEL
Give me your hand, lean on your knees—there! Good!
(the soldiers silently enter through the window)
Are we all in?

BONLARRON
Yes!

JOEL
Then before introducing ourselves into the citadel, cut the ropes which might betray us.

BONLARRON
On the contrary—let's leave them. In case of an alert we can go back the same way.

JOEL
Never! We will conquer or we will die!

ALL
Yes, yes, yes.

BISTOQUET
Even I agree!

BONLARRON
Then cut it.

JOEL
God protect us!

(Joel and Bonlarron cut the ropes which are heard falling into the gulf, then the stage becomes dark and the tower continues to descend.)

CURTAIN

ACT IV
SCENE XI

The Platform.

When the tower has completely descended, the stage represents the platform of the citadel.

Walls, towers, drawbridges at the back.

In front of the drawbridge, a sentinel patrols. The guard station is on the side.

The city is outlined obliquely at the right.

At rise, the stage is empty. Joel, followed by his men, enter furtively from the left.

JOEL
(to Bonlarron)
Two men to garrot the sentinel.

BONLARRON
(to a soldier)
Come with me.

JOEL
You, climb the pinnacle. Here's the flag—make it float over

these walls!

BISTOQUET
Long live France.
(as he takes the flag)

JOEL
Much lower—imprudent.

BISTOQUET
Pardon, sir—it's the joy of being a hero!
(he runs to the pinnacle)

JOEL
(to the others)
And as for us, gang, let's raise the gate! One moment! No gunshots. So as not to give the alarm! All sword in hand! It's a question of opening this gate to the Marshal.

(He rushes into the guard house. Noise of swords. Shouts.)

FIRST GERMAN SOLDIER
The enemy! To arms!

(Soldiers climb behind him.)

JOEL
(pointing to the group of assailants)
Help me. Fire!
(at the first shots, the group recoils)

JOEL
Spike the cannons! And us—head for the drawbridge.

(Four soldiers run to spike the cannons, six go with Joel to lower the drawbridge.)

CURTAIN

ACT IV
SCENE XII

The taking of Freibourg.

When the drawbridge is lowered, the outworks of Freibroug are seen and the countryside.

BISTOQUET
Lieutenant! Lieutenant!
(rushing, flag in hand)

JOEL
(taking the flag)
Give it to me! Give it to me!
(he runs to wave it feverishly over the drawbridge, shouting)
France! France! Come on, be firm, gang, the city is ours!

(Counterattack by the enemy. Joel and his companions with great difficulty contain the wave which, it seems, must overrun them. Then Petit Renaud, at the head of the Bombardiers, enters on foot, charging over the drawbridge, and lets loose a discharge of musketry which clears the passage.)

PETIT RENAUD
Hold tight, Joel!

JOEL
Petit Renaud—be bold, gang!

PETIT RENAUD
Forward.

(They crowd the enemy back into the town. French troops enter on foot across the drawbridge, preceded by fifes and drums. They defile before the bombardiers massed to the right and take up position at the back. Bugles of cavalry entering next and occupying the left. Entry of Marshal de Créqui with his Adjutant on horseback.)

ALL
Victory.

MARSHAL
Well done, my lads!

ALL
Long live the Marshal.
(thye bring the Marshal flags taken from the enemy)

MARSHAL
(to Joel)
Lieutenant Locmaria—it is you that I charge with bringing news of our victory to the King.
(to all)
Freibourg is ours, gentlemen!
Long live the King!
Long live France!

ALL
Long live the King!
Long live France!

(Acclamations, shouts and fanfares.)

CURTAIN

ACT V
SCENE XIII

The interior of an abandoned wood cutter's hut, in the Forest of Marly. A door, a window, no furniture.

MME DE MONTESPAN
(at the window)
The sound of the hunt horn is fading away—the hunt is returning to Marly. This hunt which is approaching here is forbidden to me, and from this abandoned hut, where no one suspects my presence, I've seen it pass by, through the trees, insulting me, with its fanfares and its laughter! And that woman I despatched to get news and who isn't returning—
(seeing Cateau)
Ah, at last, Well! Speak! Speak quickly!

CATEAU
(entering)
Well, Madame, in accordance with your orders, I mixed in with the curious crowd of peasants who were present at the picnic on the grass. The King appeared enchanted. He had eyes only for Mme. de Locmaria.

MME DE MONTESPAN
And then what?

CATEAU
Suddenly she fell ill—yes, after a sip of wine. And she had to be carried off rigid and pale like a dead person.

MME DE MONTESPAN
(to herself)
Come, the valet that I bribed to pour her that wine didn't cheat me!
(aloud)
And where did they take the charming patient?

CATEAU
The Spanish Ambassador himself undertook to escort her to Marly in this carriage.

MME DE MONTESPAN
The Duke of d'Alaméda—an intriguer—an enemy—that I will force to return to Madrid once I've regained power, along with the affection of the King! Meanwhile, by morning, I will have nothing to fear from my insolent rival.
(to Cateau)
Call, Honorou, let him bring the horses.

CATEAU
Yes, Madame.

(She goes to the window. Mme de Montespan goes toward the door. Joel, covered with dust appears on the sill of the door.)

JOEL
(accosting the Marquise as she is about to leave)
Ah, Madame—you are of the court, no doubt—where can I meet the hunt?

MME DE MONTESPAN
The hunt is no longer in the forest, sir, it's just returned to Marly.

CATEAU
(at the window, speaking to our unseen lackey)
Honorou, the horses. Madame is returning to Clagny!

JOEL
(explosively)
Ah! You are Mme de Montespan.

MME DE MONTESPAN
What's that to you?

JOEL
It's a lot to me!
(to Cateau)
Go away.
(with fury)
Why get out, will you?
(Cateau, terrified, obeys, Mme de Montespan wants to follow her)
Oh! You stay put, Madame!

MME DE MONTESPAN
Who are you?

JOEL
I am Joel de Locmaria!

MME DE MONTESPAN
Joel! The husband.

JOEL
Yes, the husband of she whose life you've sworn—

MME DE MONTESPAN
Me? Eh! I don't know Madame de Locmaria.

JOEL
Lie!

MME DE MONTESPAN
Sir!

JOEL
Lie I tell you! Just now, when I arrived at Saint Germain, radiant with a little conquered glory and with a return so long wished for, a devoted friend, Françoise Scarron came to me with this shriek, "Heaven is sending you to save your wife! A danger threatens here. The greatest of all—the hatred of Mme de Montespan."

MME DE MONTESPAN
Ah! It's the Widow Scarron who's betrayed me so!

JOEL
And as I was standing before her, mute, petrified, she continued, "I don't know precisely—but my intuition tells me that it's today, during the King's hunt, that the mine created by the infernal genius of the former favorite will explode beneath Aurora's feet: The hunt is in the forest of Marly; you will find this demon in her retreat at Clagny!" I didn't ask any more. I took my course by chance. Fever invaded my brain, anguish seized my breast—the image of Aurora in peril was before my eyes! In short, I lost my way and this hunt escaped me—but at least I've got you, you, by jimminy and you won't escape me.

MME DE MONTESPAN
You would lay your hand on me?

JOEL
Strike you, me! Oh, not at all—that's a case that concerns justice and the executioner.

MME DE MONTESPAN
Justice! The Executioner! You are mad!

JOEL
Mme de Fontange interfered with your plans and you had Miss de Fontange killed.

MME DE MONTESPAN
Slander!

JOEL
Don't deny it! I have proof of it!

MME DE MONTESPAN
Proof?

JOEL
See, here it is.
(he pulls from his packet the letter of Pierre Lesage which he shows her)

MME DE MONTESPAN
My letter to Pierre Lesage!
(she rushes on Joel to get back her letter)

JOEL
(terrible, raising his arm above his head and pushing Mme de Montespan away)
This paper is your death sentence, written and signed by your own hand!

MME DE MONTESPAN
Oh!

JOEL
Now, let's get it over with! You are going to tell me where I can

find my wife. If not, tomorrow I will go place this letter in the hands of the King, after declaring aloud to all the nobility of the realm, to the people of Paris, to the whole of France what it contains, so the judges at the arsenal will have to reopen the cell of Pierre Lesage or reignite LaVoisin's stake!

MME DE MONTESPAN
Why, sir, what has become of Madame de Locmaria?

JOEL
Well?

MME DE MONTESPAN
Just go ask the Duke of Alaméda.

JOEL
The Duke of Alaméda! Our protector! Our friend!

MME DE MONTESPAN
A friend who traffics in your honor! A protector who dreams of nothing less than making his protégée the Mistress of Louis XIV.

JOEL
The mistress of—my wife! Heaven and earth!
(terrible)
The proof of this infamy, the proof! Give it to me, Madame, or by the living god, I will exterminate you like a viper.

MME DE MONTESPAN
Proof? You want to speak of proof—recall the favors with which they overwhelmed you. This title, this rank which nothing justifies—this forced departure for Freibourg!

JOEL
Yes, yes! That's right, everything's becoming clear. Reason

is coming back to me—and with it the strength, the will to punish—
(going to the Marquise)
Madame, where is Alaméda? Where is the King? Where is Aurora?

MME DE MONTESPAN
All three are at the Chateau in Marly.

JOEL
Fine! And where is it, this lair?

MME DE MONTESPAN
(pointing to the road through the open window)
Twenty minutes from here—over there—on the edge of the forest.
(night comes on, little by little, towards the end of the scene)

(Joel stands in the doorway.)

JOEL
Thanks! There's your reward!
(he hurls the letter at her which she picks up)
Now Mr. Ambassador, and you, Sire, the three of us!

(He rushes out. Mme de Montespan follows him.)

CURTAIN

ACT V
SCENE XIV

The blow of Porthos.

A room in the Chateau Marly. At the back a large door giving on a gallery. Door to the left. Hidden door at the right. A table with a lighted candelabra.

ARAMIS
(emerging from the door at the left)
She's sleeping. And it's her rival who delivered her to us like this. Her rival who, thinking to pour her death, poured her a sleeping potion.
(sitting at the table)
Poor child! Let the King come quickly! I won't have to repent of my cowardice.
(rising)
My cowardice! Yes, my old companions in glory would reproach me with cowardice, me, their last survivor, if they knew I was trafficking in the honor of a woman—!

But those heroes didn't know any other road than the grand highway. They would be lost in the tortuous paths I've trod without them, supported by a super-human ambition. It's necessary that I be master of this Aurora, so that she will put into the hands of the King, the pen which with a stroke, scratch the heretics out from the book of human rights. Then only will the

holy company of whom I am the leader, shine all powerful over its overthrown enemies! To the chief of this henceforth invincible army, it's not a helmet but a tiara! Who cares then, who cares for the mud on the road and the broken branches under his feet as he marches to conquer the world.
(a pause, then lending his ear)
Oh! Oh! What's that? They're marching—would it be in the gallery?
(he listens in the back)
No, it's in the passage guarded by Boislaurier.
(he goes toward the door at the right)
In that case, nothing to fear! That can only be him!
(He rises from the table, the door at the right opens abruptly and Joel appears.)

ARAMIS
(recoiling)
You.

JOEL
Yes, me!

ARAMIS
But you have a post with the army—to desert is a grave mistake.

JOEL
Sir, I have nothing more to do in the army! Freibourg is taken!

ARAMIS
Freibourg is taken?

JOEL
(emphasizing)
Taken by me! In my pocket I have Marshal Créqui's report which attests to it. But that's not what it's all about. You are astonished, aren't you, to find me before you? Just now when I

came out of the forest, a providential piece of luck wanted me to see you at this window. Under this window, there opened a door before which your damned soul Boislaurier watched! I realized it was there that I would succeed in reaching you.

ARAMIS
And Boislaurier? Boislaurier?

JOEL
I think I twisted his neck for him.

ARAMIS
Wretch!

JOEL
That's a score I'm ready to settle with whoever has the right, once we've settled ours.

ARAMIS
(haughtily)
Do we have a score to settle together? Well, so be it—later I will hear you, but this is neither the time nor the place. Do you know that you are in the home of the King of France?

JOEL
By Jove! Since I am coming here to demand my wife from him!

AURORA
Your wife?

JOEL
My wife, who is here, somewhere, sleeping—sleeping through treachery, to take all conscience from her of the outrage that, but for my unexpected visit, was going to be consummated on her.

ARAMIS
Well, yes, your wife is here—but not asleep, dead!

JOEL
If I believed that, Duke, you would already no longer exist! And if it were so, there wouldn't be enough blood in you, removed drop by drop, enough flesh torn blade by blade, to expiate the crime! But your interest guarantees the contrary to me! The King isn't purchasing a cadaver from you.

ARAMIS
What! You know!

JOEL
I know you had me married to make me the husband of the favorite! I know you had me sent to Freibourg in the hope that I wouldn't return.
(gesture by Aramis)
I know, yes, I know, that you were counting on the balls of the enemy to rid you of a poor devil stupid enough not to compromise with honor.

ARAMIS
Young man, young man, if you know all that, it's really not very bright of you to come tell that. And then, did you really think, to be agreeable to you, I was going to renounce to you, I was going to renounce my plans with a gay heart? No, right—well, what do you want!

JOEL
I want my wife!

ARAMIS
Consider, in that case, to reduce me to this role, nothing less than a reason of state—necessary, imperious policy! You are a lad of wit! Don't torment like that, the hilt of your rapier—understand

me a little—let's greet each other like men of good company and return to the army where, they say you will become a great captain!

JOEL
I want my wife!

ARAMIS
Chevalier, your stubbornness will not force me to deviate from my goal! The King is going to come. Once more, get out of here!

JOEL
I want my wife!

ARAMIS
Oh! Oh! Now you are tiring my patience. Are you going to force me to kill you?

JOEL
Oh! If you were not an old geezer!

ARAMIS
(standing up)
An old geezer! Watch out, sir, watch out. At this moment you are closer to the tomb than I!
(he presents the point of his sword)

JOEL
(unsheathing his in turn)
Ah, by jimminy, we are going to see about that!
(they attack each other, the battle is prolonged, furious, silent)

AURORA
(appearing at the door to the left)
Ah! Those swords clashing. Joel! It's him! It's my Joel!
(at this moment, the young man's gaze leaves that of his adver-

sary, the latter profits to give him several rapid and severe blows which pin him to the wall)

ARAMIS
Ah! This time I've got you, my fine bird! And I am going to practice the blow of Porthos' friend on you.

JOEL
Porthos—my father.

ARAMIS
His father!
(he recoils, horrified)

AURORA
(rushing in and surrounding Joel in her arms)
Ah! Strike him now!

ARAMIS
(motionless)
The son of Porthos! Porthos, the titan, my last friend dead through my fault! Athos, D'Artagnan, my friends, my brothers, inspire me! Am I going to sacrifice the son, after the father, to my execrable ambition? Oh, no, no—I won't be a wretch to that degree.

JOEL
What are you doing, Duke?

ARAMIS
(advancing towards him)
Child, I was once known as Aramis.

JOEL
Aramis!

ARAMIS
And I am the last survivor of the four companions who took for the devise—all for one! One for all!

JOEL
It is possible! Aramis, the friend of my father!

ARAMIS
In my arms.
(he extends his arms; Joel casts himself into them, light and uproar in the gallery)
That uproar! The King already!

ARAMIS and JOEL
The King!

ARAMIS
(looking with kindness at Joel and Aurora)
Ah! What am I to do? What am I going to say to him? Who will come to my aide?

FRANÇOISE
(entering by the door at the right)
Me!

ARAMIS
Madame Scarron!

JOEL and AURORA
Our friend!

FRANÇOISE
Yes, your friend who's going to try to save you with the assistance of powerful allies who are there.
(pointing to the door at the right)

(Aramis takes a step to the side.)

FRANÇOISE
Stay, Duke.
(to Joel)
Go, rejoin them, go Chevalier. Remain with them and don't come back except at my call! Oh—don't ask any questions, have confidence in me and do what I tell you. Go!

(Joel bows and leaves to the right.)

ARAMIS
(low to Françoise)
What are you going to do, Madame?

FRANÇOISE
Receive His Majesty in your place! Do good to these children, even more perhaps—if you want me to help you!
(changing tone)
Señor d'Alaméda, we have the same faith, the same interests, we are soldiers in the same cause; will you sign a treaty of alliance with me?

ARAMIS
It is signed, Madame! And it has to succeed—for here is the King—

(The door at the back opens. The gallery can be seen filled with courtiers.)

THE KING
(turning toward the courtiers and bowing)
Good night, gentlemen. God protect you!

FRANÇOISE
Sire, I beg Your Majesty not to dismiss anyone and on the

contrary to let everyone enter.
(she goes to the door at the right and makes Joel enter, followed by Petit Renaud, Bonlarron and Bistoquet bearing enemy flags)

THE KING
Madame Scarron here.
(severely)
What's this mean?
(to Françoise)
Who are these men?

FRANÇOISE
Sire, four faithful subjects of Your Majesty: the Chevalier de Locmaria, and an officer and two soldiers of the Army of Marshal Créqui.

THE KING
So be it: but still why do I find them in my home?

FRANÇOISE
(with energy, approaching the King)
Like myself, Sire, they went to Saint Germain and you weren't there! Then, careful of your glory, I took it upon myself to bring them here, because it was necessary that they see the King.
(changing tone, softly)
And I hoped to discuss with Your Majesty, a great surprise which can only be agreeable to his great soul of sovereign and soldier.

THE KING
A surprise?

FRANÇOISE
(to Joel)
Chevalier, announce to the King the news Marshal Créqui charged you to transit to him.

JOEL
(advancing to the King and bending his knee)
Sire, I have the honor of informing Your Majesty of the surrender of Freibourg.

THE KING
Freibourg is ours?

PETIT RENAUD
Freibourg is yours, Sire.

THE KING
(to his courtiers)
Do you hear, gentlemen? Freibourg has capitulated!

JOEL
Here's the handwritten report in which Marshal Créqui gives an account to the King of the circumstances which led to the happy result of the campaign.

(The King takes the report and rapidly peruses it.)

BONLARRON
(to Petit Renaud)
Hey, Captain, were we smart to escort friend, Joel? We are looking the sun in its face!

PETIT RENAUD
Yes, I'm not sorry to make the acquaintance of the King, Godsbelly! He's around my height. Perhaps that's why they call him Louis the Great!

BISTOQUET
It's certain.

BONLARRON
Shut up, solder Bistoquet.

BISTOQUET
(pointing to his chevrons)
Call me corporal!

THE KING
(to Joel)
Here's what's best! Marshal Créqui informs me of some considerable obligations we have incurred to you. It's your turn to inform us in what way we may we can discharge this debt.

FRANÇOISE
Sire Mr. de Locmaria neither wishes nor demands but a single thing; to be returned to the affection of his young wife and be able henceforth, far from the court to consecrate himself completely to her happiness.

THE KING
Far from the court?

JOEL
Very far, Sire!

ARAMIS
(low to His Majesty)
Your Majesty understands that it is not possible to give to the conqueror of Freibourg sorrow and shame in exchange for the laurels, the flags and the glory he is bringing to his prince!

THE KING
Sir!

ARAMIS
(to Aurora)

Come on, Madame, take from the hands of these brave men the flags conquered by your spouse. The King allows you to place them at his feet.

AURORA
(bending her knee before the King)
Sire—
(she places the flags given her by Bonlarron and Petit Renaud at eh King's feet)

THE KING
(to Aurora after a pause)
Rise, Madame—and receive our goodbyes.
(to Joel)
Count—

PETIT RENAUD
Count!

THE KING
We name you governor of our lands and Chateau at Belle Isle.

JOEL
(bowing)
Ah, Sire—

THE KING
You will leave tomorrow for your government!

JOEL
(joyous, taking Aurora's hand)
Yes, tomorrow, Sire—

CURTAIN

TO PROVINCIAL DIRECTORS

In theaters which lack the means to show the scaling of the tower by the Bombardiers (Scene X), the same effect can be obtained by cutting the scene and having the Bombardiers enter through the window.

Thus, in Scene X—

JOEL
(at the window)
The ladders are attached. Are you ready?

VOICES
We are ready!

JOEL
Then, pay attention. Muskets on your back.
(confused noises below)
Look up not down—do not think of danger—thank of France.

A VOICE
Of France!

JOEL
That's the voice of Bonlarron!

BONLARRON
(appearing at the window)
Present, Lieutenant!
(turning)
Hoist, Bistoquet.

BISTOQUET
(appearing at the window)
Here I am, boss—
(sings)
In love and in war—

The Bombardiers all continue to enter using the words in Scene X. When they are all in, they leave in good order under the command of Joel. After their exit the scene change will, to the extent possible, show the platform of the fortress.

ABOUT THE AUTHOR

Frank J. Morlock has written and translated many plays since retiring from the legal profession in 1992. His translations have also appeared on Project Gutenberg, the Alexandre Dumas Père web page, Literature in the Age of Napoléon, Infinite Artistries.com, and Munsey's (formerly Blackmask). In 2006 he received an award from the North American Jules Verne Society for his translations of Verne's plays. He lives and works in México.